How to be Successful in Business

A Simple Guide to More Money, Time and Happiness

Brent Howard

How to be Successful in Business: A Simple Guide to
More Money, Time and Happiness
Copyright © 2012 Brent Howard

All rights reserved. No part of this book can be
reproduced without the prior permission of the author.

FIRST EDITION

Printed in the United States of America

Acknowledgments

I want to thank my Mother and Father for always being there for me.

I want to thank my wife, Lisa, for loving me and giving me her straight forward thoughts.

I want to thank my daughters (Chrystal and Cassidy) for always being in my life.

I want to thank my sister (Lori) for help keeping BHI Bookkeeping, Payroll and Income Tax thriving. Our clients very much appreciate her caring ways.

I want to thank my best friends, Steve and Laurie Clemens, for always being there for me.

I want to thank all of my coaches (Nate Smith, Stevenson Brooks and Nina Lewis) for their help.

I want to thank Dan Nitchie for standing by my side over all of these years at BHI Bookkeeping, Payroll & Income Tax.

I want to thank Nina Lewis for her help on creating the cover of this book.

I want to thank Marianne Thompson for her help in editing this book.

I want to thank you for reading this book.

CONTENTS

Foreward 1

Business Secret #1 4

Successful People Read 4

Business Secret #2 11

Why Are You Doing This? 11

Business Secret #3 13

S.M.A.R.T. Goals 13

Business Secret #4 19

Mission and Vision Statements 19

Business Secret #5 23

One Page Strategic Plan 23

Business Secret #6 29

Manage Your Business through Documented Systems 29

Business Secret #7 33

Implement Training Programs for your Team Members 33

Business Secret #8 39

Differentiate your Business 39

Business Secret #9 44

Market your Business Always 44

Business Secret #10 48

Implement your Marketing Plan 48

Business Secret #11 53

Create a Sales Process 53
Business Secret #12 56
Relationship Marketing 56
Business Secret #13 60
Social Media Marketing 60
Business Secret #14 75
Broken Windows - Broken Business 75
Business Secret #15 80
Five Ways to Massive Profits 80
Business Secret #16 85
Customer or Client Lists 85
Business Secret #17 90
Coaches, Consultants and Mentors 90
Business Secret #18 95
One Small Niche Business 95
Business Secret #19 100
Sell on Value - Don't Sell on Price 100
Business Secret #20 104
U.S.P. – Unique Selling Proposition................ 104
Business Secret #22 112
Strategize your Business for Generation Y 112
Business Secret #22 115
Ancient Secrets to Wealth 115
Business Secret #23 118
8 Ways to Great.. 118

Business Secret #24 122
Hire Slow, Fire Fast 122
Business Secret #25 127
Test Team Members before Hiring 127
Business Secret #26 131
Balance Personal and Business Happiness to Get the Most Out of Your Life 131
Business Secret #27 136
Fully Understand Your Accounting.................. 136
Business Secret #28 142
Become Excellent at Selling 142
Business Secret #29 153
Be a Leader 153
Business Secret #30 162
Positive Reinforcement.................................... 162
Business Secret #31 166
Results-Based Advertising.............................. 166
Business Secret #32 176
Just Do It 176
About the Author... 179
BRENT D. HOWARD...................................... 183
REFERENCES 189

FOREWARD

Thank you for taking your time to open this book and start reading it. You are already on your way to having a more successful business! The business success secrets in this book came from research I have been doing my entire 35 years in business. I've prepared and studied over a thousand bookkeeping client's records and then interviewed them to find out why they were successful, or not.

Over the last two years, I have read and studied 311 marketing and management books in my effort to understand more fully How to be Successful in Business. Then I hired a business coach, a marketing coach, a social media and sales coaches to help me make sense of all of the ideas that I learned to help businesses be successful.

Information from 53 of those books that are vital to the success of your business is included in these pages. I have quoted some very important points out of these books, but each book has more in depth explanations to offer of these important ideas. All of the titles are listed on my website at www.Las-Vegas-Business.Com.

There are 32 different chapters in this book and each one has a different *Business Secret* topic. Each chapter gives specific ideas that you can implement to make your business more successful. Try reading a chapter a day and think of how these ideas would positively help your business. Or you could read it completely then go back and read each chapter individually. The book was designed to be a fast read – about the same amount of time as going to a movie.

The challenge that we all have is the time that we think it will take. Don't try to do everything all at once. Work on the ideas that you think will have the most positive effect for your business. When you get the first idea completed, work on the second most positive effect and so forth. Many of these ideas are simple to put in place.

Millions of dollars were spent in research for the books that I read. These ideas are well-tested and not just my ideas. Please consider this as you read the book. My experience and research to better my businesses is a great reason for you to read this and put them into practice today.

The business world is changing very quickly. Don't blame any business failures on the recession, unemployment or the overall economy. Get involved and make your business stand out and new customers will be drawn to you.

Out of David Tyreman's book, *World Famous*, there is a great quote:

"There are masses of people just waiting to do business with you once they are so inspired."

Start Reading and Implementing.

Get Ready for your Business Success Now!

BUSINESS SECRET #1

SUCCESSFUL PEOPLE READ

You might say that you don't have time to read and I really understand that. I know the challenges that life has thrown me over the years and there sure were a lot of reasons that I've put aside no time to read. When I graduated early from the University of Nevada – Las Vegas (UNLV) in 3 1/2 years, I never wanted to pick up another book again. I didn't for many years.

Some studies have shown that 80% of adults will never open up a book again after they graduate from high school. Wow! Why do we do this? Maybe we think we can get the knowledge we need or want from television, radio or the internet. It doesn't sound like a bad idea, but we either forget or don't realize that these *for profit* media sources tend to **not** point out important details that might offend their audience which, in turn, affects their profits.

Years after college, I started to do some reading to help me play the guitar better. Later on,

I became a much better player with the help of an instructor's interpretations. From about 1988 until 1996, I coached my daughter, Chrystal, in girls basketball, soccer and Bobby Sox softball. To be a better coach, I read books on how to coach more effectively. Reading not only helped me, but others around me as well.

In 1992, I had been operating BHI Bookkeeping, Payroll and Income Tax (BHI) for 14 years. Even though I was very successful, I had lost a group of clients to a large CPA firm named Arthur Anderson. The internet was not as developed during that period of time, so I went to the UNLV library and searched through magazine periodicals. I found several companies that were advertising that they could help accountants get more clients. I decided on a company named New Clients Inc. from New Jersey and attended their week-long seminar in November 1993. I read all of their amazing information and implemented it. I built my business into a million dollar practice that grew from 1 to 17 employees. We've helped over 400 small businesses here in the Las Vegas valley. It's interesting to note that the same clients who left me before decided to come back years later and are still clients of mine to this day.

Unfortunately, in 1997, my first wife and I decided to get divorced. For some reason, I did not seem to get the right representation and went through several lawyers. I started to read everything about divorce and child custody law. Ultimately, I represented myself in court and created my own documents with the help of a paralegal. I found through gaining knowledge about the process that I fared better representing myself in court than with the help of an attorney.

It became a catalyst for me to become interested in government and politics. First, I built my knowledge by watching cable news show, political interviews and the Las Vegas Review Journal. After some time, I began to notice conflicting ideas that had been presented to me through these media sources. I started to read an assortment of books (popular and unpopular) about politics or government that talked about ideas and facts that didn't seem readily available to me in the media. I enjoyed learning about other important details that were otherwise not being presented to the public at large.

In 2001, frustrated with the status of personal and business rights here in Las Vegas, I ran for Nevada State Assembly. I had been a lifelong Democrat and expected when I decided to run, the local Democratic Party would help me in becoming an effective campaigner. I was surprised to find out that I would get no help at all. Once again, I turned to books, learning how to run an effective political campaign. The information I learned helped me a lot since I could get it in no other way.

One of my old classmates and friends, Bob Beers, who I've known since our 1975 band class at Clark High School, saw I was running for office and called me. At the time, Bob was a Nevada State Assemblyman. He gave me some amazing insights about how to knock on doors to meet voters and run a campaign. Bob is now a Las Vegas City Councilman.

Reading combined with some kind of coach, instructor or mentor will enable you to meet your goals.

Through my political travels, I met a very knowledgeable thinker named Elmer Chowning. He helped me understand how to combine the information I gathered by reading books on running a campaign and his insights on how our Las Vegas political system worked. In 2006, when running for Nevada Assembly for the third time, I was tied with 10 days to go before the election took place. I came so close to winning, but lost again.

In 2010, I ran into problems with my Clark County Assessor appraisal values with the five properties that I owned or was named as the trustee. The economy had tanked. Where were these inflated housing values coming from? The Assessor's office told me to read the Nevada statutes. Of course I read them, and began using the information in my formal appeals to lower values and property taxes. I kept losing the appeals though. I decided to run for Clark County Assessor as an Independent and at the same time, filed a lawsuit against the Assessor's Office in district court using those five properties as an example of how property taxes were being assessed inaccurately. I prepared the lawsuit with the help of a lawyer and, for the second time, represented myself in court. I could not find a lawyer who wanted to represent me at a price I could afford.

Clark County District Court Judge Douglas E. Smith heard the two lawyers representing the Assessor's office and didn't give me a chance to plea my case. He threw my court case out in 5 minutes flat. WOW!

I had created a website about the problems with the Clark County Assessor and how I would solve them if elected. Even though I generated a lot of traffic to my website and received some calls, I was not getting enough traction from the voters. I involved myself in several public debates but still, no traction.

On Father's Day, Chrystal gave me a $50 gift card to Barnes and Noble. By this time, I knew my campaign was missing something. Maybe I could find a book to help get my message across in a better way. I went to the store and got a book on local online marketing. It really opened up my eyes and I tried some of the ideas. On election day, I received 15,000 votes. I thank all of those voters who stood up for our rights. Even though I lost the race, I came up with a valuable idea - to start reading marketing and management books to help the three accounting businesses I managed.

As of this printing, I have read 311 marketing and management books. They are listed on my website at www.Las-Vegas-Business.com. The common characteristic of every successful person is that *they read*. They have bookshelves full of them.

Here are some ideas on how to read and understand your books:

- Write in your books. They are yours.
- Try circling the very wordy sections of the books that you want to remember.
- Turn over the corner of the page that has graphics or notes that you have written in your book.
- Get 5" x 8" index cards and write notes on the card as you read the book. You won't remember the information if you don't. By reading index cards with your notes on them, in only takes a few minutes to recall all of the important newly acquired information.

- Reach out to the author if you have questions. Go on their website for more information. Order other books written by them.

    Start reading today to become more successful.

BUSINESS SECRET #2

WHY ARE YOU DOING THIS?

Are you working in your business because you really like your business? Do you like the people you work with? Do you like the atmosphere? Do you like the vendors that you have to work with? Do you like your clients or customers? Do you earn enough money? Would you earn more money working for someone else? Do you work too many hours? Do you smile at your business? Do you enjoy the challenge of running your own business? I am sure there are other questions to ask yourself. So ask yourself!

If you answered with too many no's, then change what bothers you. You are in charge. If you can't change what bothers you, close or sell your business and start again.

You will never be as successful as you can be without enjoying what you do.

Tony Hsieh is the CEO and founder of Zappos.com which is now located here in the Las

Vegas area. The first business he started while a student at Harvard was called Link Exchange. When Tony was 24 years old, he sold it to Microsoft for $265 million dollars. Why did he sell it? He didn't like the people that he worked with. Tony then formulated his Zappos shoe-selling idea and built it around people that he liked working with in a fun atmosphere that he and his fellow team members enjoy working in. Zappos has a free tour to show off how they run their business and to give you ideas on how to run yours. Don't miss the tour. They even give you a free book to take home with you.

Go to Zappos.com to schedule your free tour. Find out for yourself why they are consistently listed in the top best companies in America to work for. Read *Delivering Happiness* by Tony Hsieh to learn more on how he created this most successful business with great people that he likes working with.

You've got to focus on your business to be successful. Don't get distracted with an atmosphere of conflicting team member personalities. They will bring you down and won't allow you to give your best to your business.

BUSINESS SECRET #3

S.M.A.R.T. GOALS

A study was done on Harvard graduates about their financial success 25 years after graduation. This study started in the early '70s and ended in the late '90s. Upon graduation, the students were asked if they had verbal, written, or both verbal and written goals. The study then followed up with these graduates 25 years later to find out what financial success they'd had.

Only 3% of the Harvard graduates answered that they had both verbal and written goals that they had followed over those 25 years. Those graduates were earning 10 times the annual income of the rest of those studied, and amazingly, had 97% of the wealth of the entire group. Wow! Do you understand the importance of setting goals?

To be successful and accomplish your dreams, goals cannot be vague. Goals like losing more weight, making more money, or to be happier in your life just won't happen without conviction. Last year I learned from Nate Smith at ActionCOACH, a nationwide franchised system of coaches created by Bradley Sugars, what S.M.A.R.T. goals are and how to use them.

I implemented my S.M.A.R.T. goal on New Year's Day this year with the purpose of losing 26 pounds in 13 weeks. I lost 27.5 pounds. I lost another six pounds in the next 13 weeks using my S.M.A.R.T. goal philosophy. I am pleased with the results. This procedure can be used for anything that you want to accomplish, and especially for business success.

On page 16 is a copy of my health S.M.A.R.T. goal chart that I taped to my bathroom mirror. Every day, I marked off what I'd accomplished for that day. Every time I marked off one of my daily goals, I patted myself on the back, or you could say that I gave myself positive reinforcement. Everyone enjoys being told that they have done something good! More importantly, what matters more is that you've told yourself you've done something good.

S.M.A.R.T. stands for:

- S – **Specific**: You must have an exact idea of what you want to accomplish.
- M – *Measurable*: You need to be able to measure your actions to accomplish the goal and the final specific goal itself.
- A – **Attainable**: It needs to be a goal that you can reasonably accomplish. If you make the goal too big and too soon, you will probably not make it happen.
- R – **Results**: There has to be an outcome that you are looking to accomplish.
- T – **Time**: There needs to be a specific time that this goal should be accomplished by. If there is no deadline to accomplish your S.M.A.R.T. goal, you probably won't get it accomplished.

Health Goal – What = Lose 2 Pounds per week = 26 Total Pounds

S.M.A.R.T Goal

- **Specific** – Lose 26 Pounds – 2 Pounds per Week
- **Measurable** – We are measuring losing 26 pounds, # of Exercise, # of Shakes, # of Salads, # of No Alcohol, # of No Fast Food, # of No FF, Bread and # of No Snacks, KPI
- **Attainable** – Lose 26 Pounds, Exercise – 5 times a Week, Shakes – 10 times a week, Salads – 1 time a week, No Alcohol – 1 time a week, No Fast Food – 4 times a week, No FF, Bread – 4 times a week, No Snacks – 4 times a week. These Action Goals can all be met with some will power
- **Results** – All of these Action Goals are Results Driven
- **Time** – All of these Action Goals Have Specific Time to be measuring them by
- **Why** – To feel better, live longer and to be there for my family. To have more energy to be more effective in business
- **How** – Goal can be attained by meeting KPI Weekly

Challenges to Accomplishing Goal

- Remember that when it is late at night and you do not feel like you have the energy to exercise that once you start exercising you will have the energy and it will put a smile on your face
- Remember that you eat to live and not live to eat
- Remember that you don't need to keep spending so much time reading and learning. You can't do much with the knowledge if you are not physically fit
- Remember that you will have a bigger smile on your face from exercising that from eating
- Get out and dance at least once a week
- Get out and play racquetball once a week
- Use the shake weight at least 3 times a week
- At the gym start pumping weights 2 times a week
- Don't get discouraged when weight does not come off quickly
- Remember you can and will accomplish this goal
- Remember you only have the Health and Marketing Goal

KPI – Key Performance Indicators

Actions	1/6	1/13	1/20	1/27	2/3	2/10	2/17	2/24	3/3	3/10	3/17	3/24	3/31
# of Exercise													
# of Shakes													
# of Salads													
# No Alcohol													
# No Fast Food													
# No FF, Bread													
# No Snacks													
My Weight	235												

My Weight on December 31, 2011

On the chart, you'll notice on the lower left hand side under Key Performance Indicators (KPI) in the Actions category that I listed Exercise, Shakes, Salads, No Alcohol, No Fast Food, No French Fries or Bread, and No Snacks. These were my Key Performance Indicators to reach my health S.M.A.R.T. goal.

I also wanted to state in the S.M.A.R.T. goal section **why** I was working towards my goal so I could read and reinforce it in my mind every day. A section could be added to include **how** you're going to accomplish the goal. This chart was customized for me specifically, but you can create your own Key Performance Indicators for you to monitor daily.

Thirteen weeks, quarterly, is a reasonable amount of time to reach your goal. Take the measurable amount of your goal and divide it by 13 weeks. The result is what you need to do every week to meet your quarterly goal. I divided my goal of losing 26 pounds by 13 weeks which equaled 2 pounds per week. This was certainly attainable because most people are able to lose about 1 pound per day when convicted to their diet.

My Key Performance Indicators were not impossible to meet. I left a couple of days a week that I didn't have to follow my daily goals. That way I could still feel positive movement toward my goal.

I also liked to list what the challenges were right up front to accomplishing my goal. This helped me really understand what I was up against. Remember, your goals have to stretch your abilities to mean something significant to you.

Start planning your own S.M.A.R.T. goals today and get ready for great success in whatever you want to accomplish.

BUSINESS SECRET #4

MISSION AND VISION STATEMENTS

The Vision Statement of your business needs to be something that is relatively short and explains how your business will help your customers. It should be explained like an overview of the direction that your company should be going.

The Mission Statement of your business will explain in more detail how you will accomplish your Vision Statement. This Mission Statement can be several paragraphs or more.

Mission and Vision statements are the goals of the company and how your business relates to your customers, vendors and team members. It is critical to your overall success. If you don't have a plan, how are you ever going to accomplish your goal? Like the old proverb states, if you fail to plan, you are planning to fail.

On the next page, you will see the Vision and Mission statements for my business. I created it as a simple one-page art piece. I then took it to a sign printer and had it mounted on a poster-size foam board.

It's displayed prominently at my office for all customers and team members to see, read and understand.

BHI Bookkeeping, Payroll and Income Tax

Our Vision Is:

Helping Businesses Profit and Grow through Implementing effective Marketing, Operational and Accounting Systems

Our Mission:

BHI is a team of committed, positive and successful people who strive to provide high quality, creative, results-oriented services for individuals and businesses, and serve as a primary resource and partner in all aspects of clients' businesses.

We take a genuine interest in our clients and team members. We understand their objectives and meet them by exceeding their expectations. We live by our values, for our clients, we will work hard and provide superior business services in a timely, effective and efficient fashion, and maintain the highest standards of professional integrity. We will foster an enjoyable working environment, based on open communication and mutual respect, and will encourage initiative, innovation, teamwork, and loyalty. Our team is proud to work and live by our 14 points of Culture.

All clients that are touched by **BHI** will benefit greatly and in some way move closer to becoming the person they want to be and achieve their most ambitious goals. Our clients will have a desire to have us help them in achieving their goals and be able to take on OUR COMMITMENT to them by returning THEIR COMMITMENT to us. They will be forward thinking, willing to learn and grow, and be willing to work as a team player in the development of their organization.

Our clients will be selected and will want to work with us because we understand people are important and systems should run a company. We offer the most practical, most applicable and fast strategies on PROFIT and GROWTH and most importantly because we mean what we say. We will give people back their spirit and freedom through business development.

We desire to measure success for our clients through awareness, increased sales, or other criteria mutually agreed upon. We are committed to maintaining a rewarding and fun environment in which we can accomplish our mission. We relentlessly pursue breakthrough ideas for our services.

By maintaining these objectives we shall be assured of a fair profit that will allow us to contribute to the community that we serve.

This wasn't the easiest project to create. I searched in Google for vision and mission statements that other companies had already created. I looked for ideas that seemed to relate to my company and what I thought would make us special and stand out from other accounting firms. I wrote several drafts and shared my ideas with Nate of ActionCOACH and this was what we came up with.

Start making one for your business today.

BUSINESS SECRET #5

ONE PAGE STRATEGIC PLAN

What is a One Page Strategic Plan?

The idea was used by tycoon John D. Rockefeller as a consistent application to help him with his success. I learned about this in a book called *Mastering the Rockefeller Habits* by Verne Harnish. This book outlines exactly how to create your one-page strategic plan and why it is important.

This is what you must do to increase the value of your growing firm. Put all of the important goals, strategies, Mission & Vision Statements, S.W.O.T. Analysis, culture values, your purpose, elevator speech and much more on one page. It should be displayed where it is easy for you and your team members to see and use.

Your S.W.O.T. Analysis is very important. This helps you figure out what you should be focusing your efforts on.

S.W.O.T. stands for:

- S – ***Strengths:*** What are the strengths of your business? This is what differentiates you from other businesses like you. Keep making them better and better.
- W – ***Weaknesses:*** Whatever your weaknesses are, you need to fix them with the goal of turning them into your strengths.
- O – ***Opportunities:*** What can you work on to make your business even better?
- T – ***Threats:*** Whatever the threats are to the success of your business, try to find ways to neutralize them.

Write out in a quick manner your **why** or **purpose** for being in this business. If *why* is a tough question to answer and does not come to you spontaneously, your success will be limited or non-existent.

Where do you see your business in three to five years? Be specific. How else will you get there? What do you want to have happen to your business in one year? What actions are you going to take in the next 90 days to get you closer toward your ultimate goal? We have already talked about S.M.A.R.T. goals and their importance. Think about this when you are making out your One Page Strategic Plan.

To remain competitive you need:

1. Framework that identifies and supports your corporate strategy.
2. A common language in which to express your strategy.
3. Well-developed habits of using this framework and the language to continually evaluate your strategic progress.

As you manage your one-page strategic plan, you need to think of it as 1% vision of your goals and 99% alignment of your team members to your goals. Remember that priority one is to get the right people in and the wrong people out.

Write your top five priorities in your one-page strategic plan, but keep talking about your first priority until it is accomplished. *Then and only then should you go on to your second priority.* Find lots of interesting ways to develop the same message. Try telling a story.

There are three basic questions in implementing your one-page strategic plan:

1. Do we have the *right* people?
2. Are we doing the *right* things?
3. Are we doing those things *right*?

Try selling a job applicant with the same vigor that you sell a new customer. You will get better team members.

Here is the team member delegation four-step process:

1. Pinpoint what they are to do.
2. Create a measurement system to monitor progress.
3. Provide feedback.
4. Give out timely recognition and rewards.

What are your big hairy audacious goals (BHAG)? These are lofty 10 to 25 year goals that you have for your business. Big Hairy Audacious Goals are discussed in more detail in Business Secret #8.

What is your brand promise? What are your value-added propositions that differentiate you from the market and your competition?

What are the critical numbers that come from your Balance Sheet and your Profit and Loss statements that by knowing these numbers will affect positive change in your business?

Do you have an accountability list? This is a list of which team member is responsible for what duty. Make sure to schedule when things are supposed to happen (deadlines) and hold team members accountable when those duties don't happen.

Do you have daily and weekly measurements for your company? Do you have daily and weekly measurements for individuals that will align with your company's goals and dreams?

Here are problem-solving guidelines to follow:

- **Relevancy:** Does the issue really matter, is it of top importance, and/or is there a customer that's been affected by the hassle?
- **Address the root:** Look at the cause of the issue and not just the symptoms.
- **Focus on the *What*, not the *Who*:** You don't want to turn your search into a finger-pointing or blame game.
- **Involve all those affected:** Rather than run around getting ten explanations from ten people, put them all in the same room to get a truer picture of the entire problem.
- **Never backstab:** Never talk negatively about anyone if that person is not present.

On the next page is an example of a one-page strategic plan that was prepared for Larry's Hideaway at 3369 Thom Blvd., Las Vegas, Nevada.

Larry's Hideaway's 14 Points of Values, Beliefs and Culture That We believe In

1. Commitment - Be Passionate and Determined
2. Ownership - Be Adventurous, Creative and Open-Minded
3. Integrity - Truth - Be Humble
4. Excellence - Deliver WOW through Service
5. Communication - Build Open and Honest Relationships
6. Success - Do more with Less
7. Education - Pursue Growth and Learning
8. Team Work - Build a Positive Team and Family Spirit
9. Fun - Create Fun and Enjoyment
10. Systems - Look for Systems for Solutions
11. Consistency - Always
12. Gratitude - Show Appreciation Often
13. Atmosphere
14. Embrace and Drive Change

Larry's Hideaway's Vision Statement

Gonna have Fun at Your Country Home away from Home where Y'all is # 1.

Larry's Hideaway 70 Second Elevator Speech

Hi, I'm Larry Fernandez and I'm the Possessor of the Friendliest Bar and Place to call Your Country Home away from Home. The Reason we Started our Business is the Need for a Country Bar in Vegas and that is because You'll can Now find us in your Country Home away from Home where You are #1.

(a) Larry is Cleanness, Courtesy, Service, Quality Food, Drinks, Games, Events and Music Shows to the Clientele.

Now I have Fun in our special Parties that when you can register to Win cash and awards in our Tournaments and Leagues in our Diamond Cards.

Now I have Fun Playing in our new pool table Tables Where we have our No Smoking in Vegas. You'll can now have our League in our new pool playing Pool.

Now I hope to can continue with the exciting Bands and Music from my house in Vegas. You'll can now Participate with us in our good saying Fun!

Y'all have Training on our Friendliness from Vegas wearing our best uniform to our Custody Safety to our Customers Care.

We are same Fun - Hideaway business we also build to the Greatest Customer Service Country and Country Bar now needed at the Y all for your very best You Find Fun at Larry's Hideaway.

Larry's Hideaway's 1 Page Strategic Plan

S.W.O.T Analysis

Strengths	Weaknesses	Opportunities	Threats
No Smoke Room	Off Main Road	Food Sales	IPS Cheaters
Cleanliness	No Food	Marketing	Big Blue Sister
Research - Look groups	Not Perfect Repair	New Drinks	Competition Financial Pressure
Friendly Towels	Curb Appeal	Greeting - Exits	Losing Money
Better Marketing	Constant Personal Change	Birthday Parties	Government

Purpose (Why)	Targets 3-5 years (Where)	1 Year Goals (What)	Quarterly Goals (Actions)
To Promote Profitable and Fun Times for our Guest Patrons around with other business owners	Future Date 1/1/2014 Revenue $ 900,000 Profit $ 250,000	Year End 12/31/12 Net Earning Win after Promos $ 260,000 Net Profit $ 50,000 24 New Members 200 Cash $ 20,000 Ave. Cash Sale per Cash Guest $ 20 3 Birthday Parties 300 Ave. Cash in per Week $ 200,000 Liquor Cost 30% New Guest Contact info per New Guest 10%	Qtr End 2/29/12 Net Earning Win after Promos $ 65,000 Net Profit $ 5,000 6 Club Members 200 Cash $ 10,000 Ave. Cash Sale per Cash Guest $ 25 3 Birthday Parties 5 Ave. Cash in per Week $ 60,000 Liquor Cost 30% New Guest Contact info per New Guest 20%

Actions
- Greeting Mass Tied Help Learn Team Members
- Do this Every Probable Team specific
- Well Preserved Team Members
- Daily cleaning
- Marketing - Customer Lists
- More events with 30 Team Memberships
- Maintenance all Team Members

BHAG
Big Hairy Audacious Goal

Highly Profitable and Successful business that provides excellent service and Fun.
We will be great at Gaming, Food, Drinks, Pool Leagues and Adult Birthday Parties.

Amount Numbers
- Cost for Weekly per Pre order
- Number of Club Members

Bonus Promos
You are Gonna have Fun at Your Country Home away Home, and Personal Games Where Y'all are Number 1.

Critical Numbers	Critical Numbers
1. Marketing - ROI	1. Marketing - ROI
2. Profit	2. Pay It
3. Net Earning Win	3. Net Earning Win
4. Cash Liquor & Food Sales	4. Cash Liquor & Food Sales
5. # of Larry's Team Champions	5. # of Larry's Team Champions

Quarter and Annual Theme
We have the Friendliest Personal Relationships with our Guests in Las Vegas.

When will be the Team Reward for meeting a open the Larry's Goal?

Larry's Hideaway Greeting & Guest Exit

1. Welcome each Guest with Big Smile, Eye Contact and a Handshake Hug.
2. If you know your #1 Guest's Name - Would you like your Regular or would you like to try one of my favorite Bar Name new favorite. When you ever order ask the Guest and Best call and see some Give your name where you need something.
3. If you like some Good Times My name is (Your own Name). What is your name? (Guest's Name) What is your Favorite Drink or would you like to try one of our favorite Bar? (Your favorite)
4. All are our good members cheers greet and welcome to here
5. Explain to each Guest on Friday events on Gaming or sing or similar as her
6. Every time you are willing to eat tonite or her first Fence
7. Would you like some foodies snacks nuts and chips or some Chex Mix?
8. Each Guest stops this lane with me bud Eye Contact is My name is (Your name) my owner of Guest's Name Thanks for coming in the Hideaway, I hope to see you in Class I can also hear the spread of good job

Larry's Hideaway Mission Statement
Our firm Larry's Hideaway who provides Happiness and Joy through Gaming, Spirits, Music, Dancing, Billiards at our Completely Safe Country Home away from Home where everyone feels they are #1.

We have a passion to Serve Trust the Food and Drink we sell to our guests meets the highest standards of quality, freshness and good taste. To constantly provide our customers with impeccable service by demonstrating service, graciousness, efficiency, knowledge, professionalism and integrity in our work. To have every guest who comes through our doors leave impressed our Larry's Hideaway and excited to come back again. To keep our concept fresh, exciting and on the cutting edge of the hospitality and entertainment industry.

We give exceptional attention to detail to ensure that each guest receives correct, professional, friendly and courteous service. To provide all who work with us a friendly, cooperative and rewarding environment which encourages long term, satisfying, growth employment. To maintain a clean, comfortable and well kept and attractive bar so our guests and team members who are in business to create the structure and systems needed to completely provide our remarkable Home away from Home for our guests. Our team members are to act by what and are Larry's 14 Points of Culture.

Our guests will always be greeted with our team member's name with a hand shake or a hug, Direct eye contact with a big smile, and knowledge about our guests, with team members asking guests open ended questions, with other trust suggestions for food, drink or entertainment and information about what is happening currently at Larry's Hideaway.

Every guest that chooses to leave us moves Happy will thank me, from our SMILE'n team members by their Real name and a suggestion to be seen for our guest the very next shortly.

By representing these objectives we shall be assured of a fair profit that will allow us to continue in the community that we serve.

Scoreboard Design?

BUSINESS SECRET #6

MANAGE YOUR BUSINESS THROUGH DOCUMENTED SYSTEMS

Have you ever thought about the importance of setting a goal for your business to be 10 times as big instead of just a little bigger? How will this affect the efficiency of the operation of your business?

How could you possibly handle 10 times as much business if you hang onto the responsibilities of the craftsman, manager, accountant, marketer, salesman or maintenance man? If you are a very small business, you can take care of it for a while. But when you get much bigger, you will start making more mistakes just because of your time restrictions. You will then reach out for team members to help you and find out that they normally don't have the same enthusiasm as you do for your business. Your team members mainly just want to work for you and go home. If they wanted to operate their own business they would already be doing it.

During the first 15 years of BHI, I did almost all of the bookkeeping, payroll preparation and income tax preparation. I did a great job and made a great living. At least I thought I did. The problem was that if I got an additional client, I would ultimately lose a client, because there just weren't enough hours in the day. I sure tried creating hours. From January 1st through April 30th of each year, I worked about 12 hours a day. I never thought about creating a system for a large company so I wouldn't have to work so hard and put in long hours. I couldn't figure out how to duplicate my efforts with the help of other people. That is a challenge I am still working on today.

The secret of successful larger businesses is that they focus on creating and refining documented business systems. They manage the system and not the team members that work into the system. There are still problems that have to be handled, however, they continue managing their system. When there is a problem, they create a new system or change an existing system to solve the problem.

One of the reasons that many franchises are successful is that they have already spent the time creating a tested documented business system that they know will bring results.

Grinding It Out: The Making of McDonalds is the book authored by Ray Kroc that helped me to understand the importance of business systems. Mac and Dick McDonald are the original creators of McDonalds hamburgers. They created a system to make sure that all food prepared came out the same every time. They had several stores already when a shake machine salesman named Ray Kroc came into their store on a sales call. Yes, he sold them several shake machines, but Kroc became excited with the business system the McDonald brothers had created to run their store.

Kroc proposed to the McDonald brothers that he could market their business and help them become a very large successful business. The McDonald brothers took Ray Kroc up on his offer and the rest is history.

It was the documented business system that helped make McDonalds so successful. Remember this when you are thinking about the amount of time that it will take to create such a system.

In today's world, there are many ways to make systems easier to present to team members. Document your business systems with the help of videos, podcasts, screen sharing, Webinars and portals on the web to easily share PDFs or documents. There are many other ways to check on the status of your system from anywhere. You could use online cameras with audio, or Point-of-Sale (POS) systems that you can manage on the web where team members can be emailed quizzes so you're assured that they have understood your systems.

Don't wait. Start today creating your documented business systems. Just maybe you can also be as successful as McDonalds.

BUSINESS SECRET #7

IMPLEMENT TRAINING PROGRAMS FOR YOUR TEAM MEMBERS

I had thought that I could just hire team members and they would know exactly how to handle procedures at my businesses with just a little coaching. I would then let them go and look after what they accomplished every now and then. As long as I was making money, everything was OK with how my team members handled their job. If not, I just fired them and started again. Many times, though, I would hold onto team members way too long in the hopes that they would just start following my direction on their own. Hire slow and fire fast is a better answer, but not a better direction to a better solution. Have you ever handled the management of your team members in this manner?

In *The Customer Comes Second* by Hal F. Rosenbluth, I learned some very important ideas. Most everyone has heard of the concept that the customer comes first. This is not really correct, because how can the customer come first if your team members don't know how exactly to treat them? Also, the customer expects to be treated in the same first-class manner that they have been treated before or they won't be coming back. Therefore, the customer comes second and the team member comes first.

But how do you get every team member to treat our valuable customers with first-class treatment every time? The secret is training. Here are some highlights from the book that will help you in your quest for top-notch training of your team members:

- Consider training an essential part of your company.
- Make Learning Fun.
- Training must be done on a regular basis.
- Consider teaching leadership skills.
- Continually sharpen your technical training and be sure it's comprehensive enough to enable you to hire people with no experience in your particular field to get up-to-speed quickly.
- Always provide training for your team members when you are adding new products, services or procedures.
- Daily coaching of your team members will strengthen their skills.

- Consider theater, teaching and corporate training backgrounds when selecting training staff.
- Involve team members throughout your business to train other employees.
- Commit the training resources necessary for your company in terms of its resources and time.

The Ritz-Carlton Hotel Company has won the Malcolm Baldridge National Quality Award twice. I haven't yet had the pleasure of staying at a Ritz-Carlton, but I am looking forward to it. To win this award, which is handed out by the President of the United States, the winner has to share their procedures with the public on how they accomplished their performance excellence. Joseph A. Michelli explains how the Ritz-Carlton achieves such high quality success at their hotels in his book entitled, *The New Gold Standard.*

    I would like to share one of the amazing ideas that Ritz-Carlton implements. Before every shift is started, all team members meet as a group. Their team leader shares the current challenges and successes happening at Ritz-Carlton. This was everyone's small training session every day. It's very effective, because without consistent conversation, it's easy to forget what is really important.

After reading this book along with other sources of information, I decided that "training" was a missing element that was hampering our success at Larry's Hideaway and Larry's Villa here in Las Vegas. I put an ad on Craigslist and hired a business trainer. She and the managers at both locations led and started our weekly meetings. Daily challenges and successes we experienced were shared and aired. Any new promotions, products, services or ideas were also mentioned. We also asked for team member's ideas on how to improve both Larry's Hideaway and Larry's Villa.

After we had been doing our weekly meetings for about six months, we started a Daily Huddle. It was impossible for everyone meet before the shift started, so each manager conducted a 15-minute conference call with all team members that were coming on shift in the next 24 hours to make sure the team had the most current information. I am presenting our Daily Huddle worksheet that our managers filled out every day on the next page.

Larry's Hideaway – Daily Huddle – Date _____ Time _____ Leader _____

When – Specific Time Every Day 15 Minutes Top – Short Conversations – Please Stand Up

Where – All Daily Huddles will be made by Phone on Conference Call and Setup will be handled by Leader.

Who – This is a mandatory phone meeting for All Team Members coming on shift in the next 24 hours.

Why – Daily Huddles help our Larry's Team by giving positive reinforcement by each Team Member by each Team Member, by keeping our Teams # 1 Focus on Greeting/Thank You, by keeping focus on the Ownership point of Larry's Culture and by keeping good, warm, constant communication between all Team Members helps align Larry's Culture with Larry's Operation.

Positive Reinforcement of Each Team Member by Each Team Member

Name _____ Statement _____

Name _____ Statement _____

Name _____ Statement _____

Name _____ Statement _____

Each Team Member verbally practices Larry's Greeting/Thank You – Leader Critics

Name _____ Perfect? What could be improved? _____

Name _____ Perfect? What could be improved? _____

Name _____ Perfect? What could be improved? _____

Name _____ Perfect? What could be improved? _____

What Ownership action was taken of Larry's Procedures by you and with whom?

Name _____ Action _____ Whom _____

Name _____ Action _____ Whom _____

Name _____ Action _____ Whom _____

Name _____ Action _____ Whom _____

What was my Last Shift's #'s, Bartender (Coin In, Change %, Comp %)? What is one action that I will take to improve these numbers?

Name _____ Coin In _____ Change % _____ Comp % _____

My Action _____

Name _____ Coin In _____ Change % _____ Comp % _____

My Action _____

Name _____ Coin In _____ Change % _____ Comp % _____

My Action _____

Name _____ Coin In _____ Change % _____ Comp % _____

What's up with you? – What's happened to you personally and at Larry's that been great?

Name _____ Personally _____ Larry's _____

Name _____ Personally _____ Larry's _____

Name _____ Personally _____ Larry's _____

Where are you stuck? What happened to you personally at Larry's that could be improved?

Name _____ Personally _____ Larry's _____

Name _____ Personally _____ Larry's _____

Name _____ Personally _____ Larry's _____

Name _____ Personally _____ Larry's _____

Please make sure to personally thank everyone on this call and do not let this go over 15 minute's total. When there items that can't be discussed in a short sentence or phrase, please discuss after the meeting. Please make sure that all issues that are brought up are taken serious and responded to within 24 hours.

Thanks,

BUSINESS SECRET #8

DIFFERENTIATE YOUR BUSINESS

Did you ever wonder why your business doesn't seem to be growing? Do you get bored or tired when you go to your favorite restaurant and even though the food is great, something nags at you, telling you to try somewhere else? Do you purchase some products or services regularly, not really caring where you get them from or which brand that you use?

When it doesn't seem to matter what brand you buy or where you buy a particular product or service, it becomes a commodity. When you buy a product that is a commodity, you will normally just buy on price or convenience. This makes for a lot of competition which also makes it more difficult for that particular business to be profitable.

Business is hard enough. What could make it easier to make a profit? The answer is to differentiate your product or service so that it is not the same as all of the other businesses in your category. You want to create a new category. When you are the first to create a new category, you are automatically the leader. You have no competition on price. It won't be boring, because it's still new to your clients.

In Jim Collins' book, *Good to Great,* he studied a large number of very successful companies to come up with what has contributed to making these companies so great. One of his ideas that I would like share with you is BHAG (Big Hairy Audacious Goals). A BHAG is the goal that you are dreaming for that is so large that it seems impossible, but it is really what you are driving all of your actions toward. It may take you years to accomplish, but it doesn't really matter to you. To help you define your BHAG, there are three questions to ask yourself. Where these three questions overlap is your BHAG.

1. What are you deeply passionate about?
2. What can you be the best in the world at?
3. What drives your economic engine?

In David Tyreman's book, *World Famous,* he helps show you how to give your business a *Kick-Ass brand identity.* Here are some of the major ideas that you can learn about in this book:

- Liberate your business from trying to please everyone.

- Have three words that will explain how your customers will benefit from your product or service.
- Your three words should be your business' personality, attitude and value.
- What is your Brand's promise?
- What is your Brand's playground?
- Every business has a brand. Even if you are very small.
- Add Psychographics to your brand. Psychographics put a face, a heart, and mind to the demographic you have chosen to do business with.
- Always look for new ways to add value.
- Work to provide a seamless and effortless experience.
- Touch people's hearts and minds.

In Seth Godin's book, *Purple Cow*, he helps show you how to *transform your business by being remarkable.* Here are some ideas to make your cow (business) purple (different):

- How could you modify your product or service so that you'd show up on the next episode of Saturday Night Live?
- Explore your limits. What if you're the cheapest, the fastest, the slowest, the hottest, the coldest, the easiest, the most efficient, the loudest, the most hated, the

- copycat, the hardest, the oldest, etc? If there is a limit, you should test it.
- Copy from other industries and put those ideas into operation in your business.
- Find things that are just not done in your industry and do them.

Ken Blanchard's book, *Raving Fans*, is an easy-read that is written as a story. It is a book about differentiating the customer service of your business so that your customers will become raving fans. The benefit of having your customers becoming raving fans is they will refer your business to their friends. This is word-of-mouth advertising and will get you the highest return on your advertising dollars of any other method you can imagine.

Everyone knows about Starbucks. In the *World Famous* book that I talked about earlier, Starbucks is used as an example. Did you realize that another group had already built a few Starbucks stores in Seattle? Howard Schultz had no experience in the coffee business. He got involved in the stores as an employee and later bought them out. He investigated coffee and created a coffee experience.

In Joseph A. Michelli's book, *The Starbucks Experience*, he tells the entire story of Starbucks. He also explains the five principles for turning ordinary into extraordinary. All of his employees have a *Green Apron Book.* It is one of Starbucks' ways to make sure that the Starbucks experience is the same at every store. After reading the book, I asked my daughter, Chrystal, who is always going to Starbucks, if she could get a copy from one of the baristas. They happily handed her one. I took the best ideas and created a document to help the bartenders at Larry's Hideaway and Larry's Villa devise a better customer experience. They signed it at every shift so I knew that they looked at it.

There are many great ideas in this book to help differentiate your business, or as Michelli said, turn ordinary into extraordinary.

BUSINESS SECRET #9

MARKET YOUR BUSINESS ALWAYS

If one leg of a three-legged stool was broken, the stool would not stand. In business, the three legs are Marketing, Accounting and Production. However, there would be nothing to account for or no production of product or service to manage if there wasn't marketing.

Did you ever consider marketing as a system? Did you think that you could just hire the radio executive to write your ads? Could you just hire the billboard's graphic artist to create your billboard ad? Did you think you could just hire the paper's graphic artist to create your ad? Did you think you were saving money by having the advertising media create your ad?

I know that I did. I have tried by hiring numerous advertising media for Larry's Hideaway and Larry's Villa and the results were not profitable. I have tried to hire an outside service to create my ads and that hasn't worked either. One of the main reasons that I have done so much studying in the last two years into business marketing and management is that I have not found the right solution yet to the growth problems of my three businesses.

I am close though.

Marketing is the most important component of your business. It is the fuel that drives your business. You need to have a written marketing system that you consistently implement and monitor for its effectiveness.

But who will create it for you?

If you work in a connected group of businesses like a franchised or licensed organization, there would be a marketing department that would create the entire system for you. You pay them for it. One of the problems with such a model is if isn't working, well, you don't have the right to change it.

You started your own business for many reasons. Maybe you didn't really understand all of the responsibilities that you have, but you have them.

Your number one responsibility is to create, implement, monitor and maintain your marketing system.

There are many consultants or coaches that can help you figure out the direction that you want your marketing system to go. Invest the money and the time to implement a highly-effective marketing system. Don't expect your employees to come up with breakthrough ideas.

In Jon Spoelstra's book, *Ice to the Eskimos*, he shows how to market a product nobody wants. Jon Spoelstra was the marketing director of several unprofitable NBA teams. He shares how he increased sales dramatically. Here are a few of his ideas that helped those NBA teams:

- The real price of getting new customers is a commitment to getting them.
- Don't delegate the marketing.
- Truly focus on new business.
- If we ran an ad in the newspaper and got $4 in ticket sales for each $1 we spent, we'd run the ad again. If not, we wouldn't.
- Companies never improve from the bottom up. The president must jump-start the marketing effort.
- Any company needs to innovate all of the time. Innovate, Innovate, Innovate!
- Only try to sell a product that the customer wants to buy.

- Try to sell the customer a little more than they wanted to buy.
- Make the client the hero and make him look good by buying.
- Raise prices and give more value.

Jon Spoelstra increased the sales of these NBA teams by hiring as much marketing staff that he could get his hands on and then monitored their effectiveness. He liked to hire self-motivated employees.

Spoelstra proved that if you focus on the marketing of your company as the number one priority, you would be successful even if you had a sub-par product to market.

BUSINESS SECRET #10

IMPLEMENT YOUR MARKETING PLAN

Marketing is the engine that propels your business success through growth. Doesn't it make sense to document what marketing actions your business will take? What media methods will you use to advertise your business? When will you implement *which* marketing campaigns? How much will you spend on each marketing method? How will you track your results?

A marketing plan is a business system. It has goals to achieve. Think about it in terms of the S.M.A.R.T. goals method that was explained earlier. Instead of trying to think every day what to do about marketing, design your plan and follow it. Constantly monitor and adjust your plan to the results that you are getting from working your marketing plan.

Dan S. Kennedy wrote a book called *The Ultimate Marketing Plan* in which he shows how to create a marketing plan. The following is a summary of the steps, principles, and ideas presented in this book to help you develop your own Ultimate Marketing Plan:

- Research your competition and similar businesses, products and services. What are their features, benefits, claims and unique selling propositions?
- What are the features and benefits of your business, product or service?
- Develop your Unique Selling Proposition.
- What is your irresistible offer?
- What are the needs of your customer?
- What is the general thing that fulfills their needs?
- Explain why your product, service or business is the best thing.
- Justify your price.
- Give the reasons your customers should act now.
- How can you build the customer's interest in your product, service or business?
- What are your calls to action? What do you want your customer to do?
- Describe your geographic target market.
- Describe your demographic target market.
- Describe your association and affinity target market.
- List all the types of pictorial proof you have.

- List all the testimonial proof you have. Do you have celebrities and real people?
- List the demonstration proof you have.
- Describe your extraordinary guarantees.
- Is the appearance of your business superb?
- Do you have a brand name identity?
- What are your charities or nonprofit connection ideas?
- What are your personal self-promotion ideas?
- How do you position yourself as an expert?
- What are your creative promotions?
- Can you get on a talk show?
- What is new in your business 30, 60 and 90 days from now?
- Set up a calendar that shows what promotions you will be implementing, and when. These can be around special holidays.
- What are your inbound telephone procedures?
- What are your telephone upsell procedures?
- What are your outbound telemarketing procedures?
- Do you have window displays?

- What is your teaser newspaper advertising?
- What are you honored guest greeting procedures?
- What is your customer retention plan?
- How are you going to earn referrals?
- Do you have sales surge activities like big discounts, sweepstakes, red-tag sales, coupons, premium give-a-ways, crazy accountant sales, sports-related promotions, trade-ins, e-z payment terms or celebrity appearances?
- Do you have procedures for marketing using new technologies like the internet, social media, text, audio brochure, video brochure, infomercials, desktop publishing, robot telemarketing and others?

Go through each one of these ideas and come up with your best answers. Document everything. Yes, this will take some time. You can't delegate this project. You can get help through coaches. Your time will be well spent on this project. Implement your Marketing Plan and watch your business grow.

The below document is a Marketing Plan/Strategy template for BHI Bookkeeping that helps calculate Return on Investment of marketing costs. It also lists marketing processes that we will be implementing.

BUSINESS SECRET #11

CREATE A SALES PROCESS

Would it be valuable to you and your business to increase your conversion rate of incoming sales leads to closed sales? Do you know what your conversion percentage of incoming sales leads to closed sales? Like everything in business, a thought-out and well-documented plan that you follow will increase your conversion rate. You can always adjust what activities you are implementing in your sales process. Do more of that activity when it works and stop doing the other activity when it doesn't work.

First, create the outline of your sales process and then create each document or promotion piece that you need to fully implement your sales process. The next step is to follow your sales process and monitor its success.

We use Sage Act as CRM (Customer Relationship Management) software to help us track where the status of our prospects are in our sales process.

On the next page, I have displayed for you our latest version of our Sales Process for BHI as an example for you.

BHI Sales Process

1. **Prospect Inbound from Marketing – CRM Stage 1** – Start a series of 9 Email Auto Responders – Put on BHI Newsletter List – Put in BHI CRM Database

2. **Contact Prospect by Phone within 48 hours – CRM Stage 2** – Attempt Appointment

3. **After Appointment Set Within 1 hour – CRM Stage 3** – Email or Fax Questionnaire, Brochure, 11 Reasons Document, Why Us Document

4. **Contact Back By Email, Fax or Phone to make sure Information was Received within 48 hours – CRM Stage 4** – Remind that Questionnaire need to be finished before appointment – Opportunity to ask more questions about the challenges that they have with their business

5. **After Questionnaire is Received within 24 hrs. – CRM Stage 5** – Send Information Package and DVD/CD. – Coach phone them to thank them for information – Opportunity to ask more questions and remind them of appointment

6. **Call to see if the Received the Information Package within 24 hours – CRM Stage 6** – Ask if they have questions about information package

7. **Sent Post Card 72 hours before meeting to remind Prospect of Meeting – CRM Stage 7**

8. **Call 24 hours before meeting to remind of meeting – CRM Stage 8**

9. **Coach attends sales meeting with prospect and completes sale – CRM Stage 9** – If no sale is completed coach calls within 72 hours to follow up

10. Send Welcome Package 24 hours after sale – CRM 10

BUSINESS SECRET #12

RELATIONSHIP MARKETING

Decades ago, we had several main forms of media to get our information from - the local newspaper, the big three television networks (ABC, NBC, CBS) and radio. Now we have the internet, hundreds of channels on cable or satellite television and satellite/high-definition radio. We used to really notice what was being advertised to us. Now, we hardly notice anything that is promoted to us. Decades ago, we had much less than 1,000 daily advertising messages directed at us. Today, there are over 5,000 daily advertising messages coming our way.

We've become de-sensitized to advertising.

Why does this matter to you and your business? It matters because you need to be able to understand your target market audience much better than your competitors in order to be successful in today's economy.

Another main reason that consumers are tuning out your message is that your message is interrupting their world. Think about the last movie or show you watched on television. When the pivotal or climactic scene was about to come up, all of a sudden, a switch goes off and several commercials are shown before the exciting moment is shared with you. This has annoyed me many times and most likely it has also annoyed you. Did you really go out and buy their product? I didn't, but enough people must be buying their product or the advertisers wouldn't keep running these ads.

Interruption marketing is the name for marketing messages that stop you from what you are doing in order to try to get you to buy their product.

The great news is that interruption marketing methods are losing their effectiveness. What should businesses do to get their message out to their target market?

Relationship Marketing is the answer. Social media is the tool to help your business create new relationships with your target market and maintain relationships with your existing customers or clients.

Mari Smith has helped me understand how to build a large, loyal and profitable network using the social web in her book entitled, *The New Relationship Marketing.* Here are some of the ideas to use from her book:

- Figure out the top 16-25 people to have a relationship with that would blow your mind.
- Follow their postings on Twitter, Facebook and LinkedIn. Occasionally comment on their postings or share them with your social network.
- "Like" their Fan Page and post on their Wall.
- Don't sell your product to them.
- Give your target market a meaningful gift by adding helpful ideas to the ideas they have stated.
- Look to klout.com to rank their online presence so you can see how well-followed a brand they are.
- Seek first to understand and then to be understood.

Here is her four-part formula for building a loyal community:

1. Build a quality network. Quantity will come later.
2. Provide quality content.
3. Be consistent.
4. Be genuine, authentic, and passionate. Show you care about them.

A quality network is made up of prospects that:

- Would be in your target market.

- Would match the criteria of your ideal client.
- Would be people that you genuinely admire and would like to meet.
- Whose books, seminars and blogs you read or subscribe to.
- You would like to build a relationship with.
- Are your peers or contacts.
- Provide a great source of news.
- Meet the needs of your audience.

Find their pain points and craft products that meet their needs. Become a human aggregator and look out for quality and unique content to share with your network. Write on blogs with visibility that pertains to your industry.

Work on discontinuing using interruption marketing and start using relationship marketing, especially through social media platforms.

BUSINESS SECRET #13

SOCIAL MEDIA MARKETING

Should social media be used for marketing? How should it be used? Who should do social media for marketing? Can it be a successful source of marketing for your business? What platforms should be used? Is your business involved in social media yet, or just you personally?

These are all great questions. As I talked about earlier, you should not engage in interruption marketing methods and instead should market by building relationships with your targets, prospects, clients and customers. Social media is a great way to build relationships.

Let me tell you a few of the actions that I have tried that have not worked so well yet.

I am on Facebook. I have about 5,000 friends and as of today that is the limit of my friends. I originally spent a lot of energy working on the premise that I just wanted to be friends with anyone in Las Vegas for several reasons. My first reason was that I was running for office and felt it was a good way to get my ideas out. The second reason was I wanted to be in contact with Las Vegas people that might be interested in BHI, Larry's Hideaway or Larry's Villa in an effort to get more clients or customers. Even though I shared many ideas with all of my friends, the results were not positive. Why? I was just trying to sell my product or ideas.

Facebook is not the platform to be selling. This is a relationship-building site. Unless you are a teenager, Facebook is not about the quantity of friends you get.

It is the quality of the relationships that you build with friends on Facebook that is most important.

Facebook Marketing: An Hour a Day by Mari Smith is a great book that can help you understand how to develop your plan of attack to marketing your business through Facebook.

Social Media Marketing: An Hour a Day by Dave Evans is also a great book that can help you understand how to build your marketing plan through social media platforms, and then how to track your return on investment through the use of social media metrics.

You should also consider getting someone in your business to be your social media marketer. An allotted amount of time should be set aside every day to build relationships with your customers. The key point here is to use the name of your business in your name. This way, when you are building relationships by adding to your customer or prospects posts, they see it. If they want to know more about what you have to sell, they can go to your website, fan page or other type of sharing site.

Twitter is an interesting platform for sharing ideas and building relationships. You can share your ideas with the followers of whomever you mention in your tweet by putting @ in front of their name, for example - @brenthowardlv. Hashtagging is a great way of sharing ideas about a certain theme. Put a # sign in front of the idea and Twitter categorizes all tweets that have the same hashtag (#bookkeeping). You now can send messages to all that have put a hashtag in one of their tweets with further information to the right of the # symbol. This is a great way of building relationships.

Twitter Marketing: An Hour a Day authored by Hollis Thomases will give you amazing details on the best way to use Twitter to get your message out and build relationships. My 20 year-old daughter, Cassidy, loves Twitter more than

Facebook because the messages are short and limited to 140 characters.

Commit to tweeting 3 times a day. Tweet for 15 minutes in the morning, 15 minutes at noon and 15 minutes at the end of the day. Remember that Twitter users will normally see the most current tweets and miss older messages or tweets.

Look for people to follow that have a lot of followers and analyze what they say interests *their* followers. Adapt their ideas into what you want to share. It's a fact that 10% of Twitter users have created 90% of the tweets. Look for the ones that are really using Twitter.

Jeffrey Gitomer wrote a book called *Social Boom! How to Master Business Social Media* that can be very helpful in designing your social media marketing plan for your business. He is quoted as saying:

The formula for business social media success: Attract people, engage people, connect people. The best way to accomplish all three is with value.

Start with information that you learned from another source and then explain why that should be important to the reader. Remember that adding insight is adding value. Work hard to be fascinating, and develop and express a distinct point of view. Stand up or don't bother. The world needs your offbeat observations, your advice and your cutting edge solutions.

Here are Gitomer's eight steps for using social media to get an audience with whoever you want:

1. Find your prospect.
2. Follow them.
3. Read their posts.
4. Collect information.
5. Listen.
6. Connect with them. Re-tweet some of their most impactful messages and add a few words of your own. Mention them in your tweets as they influenced you or helped you in your business. Tweet about their success, articles or press. Find relevant LinkedIn groups they participate in and offer intelligent answers. Answer questions your prospects are answering.
7. Reach out and direct-message them.
8. Align yourself with people that you know they follow and listen to them.

Engage is the complete guide for brands and businesses to build, cultivate, and measure success in the new web that was written by Brian Solis. Here are his rules for engagement in the social web:

- Unveil the communities of influence and discover their choices, challenges, impressions, and wants.

- Participate where your presence is advantageous and mandatory; don't just participate anywhere and everywhere.
- Consistently create, contribute to, and reinforce service and value.
- Concentrate participation where it will offer the greatest rewards for both sides.
- Assess pain points, frustrations, and also expressions of contentment to establish emotional connections.
- Determine the brand identity, character, and personality you wish to portray. Match it to the individual persona of who's in front of it when online.
- Adapt predefined personalities with the voice of the community in which you engage.
- Observe the behavioral cultures within each network and adjust your outreach accordingly.
- Become a true participant in each community you wish to galvanize.
- Don't speak at audiences through messages.
- Dig deeper to connect what transpires in the Social Web to your business objectives.
- Learn from each engagement.
- Ensure a point of contact who is ultimately responsible for identifying, trafficking, or

responding to all things that can affect brand perception.
- Act, don't just listen and placate – do something.
- Earn connections through collaboration.
- Empower advocacy.
- Embody the attributes you wish to portray and instill.
- Don't get lost in conversation or translation; ensure your involvement strategically maps to objectives specifically created for the Social Web.
- Establish and nurture beneficial relationships online and in the real world as long as public perception and action is important to your business.
- Un-campaign programs and ensure they're part of a day-to-day cause.
- Un-market by offering solutions and becoming a resource to your communities.
- Give back, reciprocate, acknowledge, add value, and contribute where it makes sense.

Master the *Art of Conversation*. Here are the steps to master:

1. I'm listening to you.
2. I hear you.
3. I understand you.
4. Take action.
5. Identify opportunities to engage with them.

6. Experience nature, dynamic, ambience and emotion of the dialogue.
7. Empathize as a peer.

Think in terms of Physiographics (attributes relating to personality, values, attitudes, interests or lifestyles). Learn about and motivate people. See and connect with those who band together through tasks, preferences, interests and passions regardless of age, gender or location.

Here are the "Five Ws" of social media that you need to master:

- **Who** – Define brand personality and what it symbolizes.
- **What** – Listen to online conversation and learn from what's said.
- **Where** – Track down where your presence is required.
- **When** – Pinpoint when your opportunities arrive. Monitor the web in real time.
- **Why** – Find the reasons that warrant your participation. Find the recurring themes, topics, questions and insights.

Then you can move on to:

- **How** – Become a part of the community.
- **To what Extent** – Identify individuals that can help you tell your story. Business-to-Business social media is comprised of 68%

spectators and 19% collectors. Only 13% are sharing.

In Seth Godin's book, *Permission Marketing*, he explains how to build business relationships by using their permission to share ideas with them. He believes that you should turn strangers into friends and friends into customers.

Here are the first steps to getting started with Permission Marketing:

1. *Figure out the lifetime value of a new customer.* Without this data it will be extremely difficult to compute what it is worth to acquire a new permission.
2. *Invent and build a series of communication that you will use to turn strangers into friends.* This must take place over time. They must offer the consumer a selfish reason to respond. The responses should alter the communications moving forward. They should have a final call to action so you can measure the results.
3. *Change all of your advertising to include a call to action.*
4. *Measure the results of each series of communication.* Throw out the bottom 60% and replace with new communication.
5. *Measure how many permissions you receive.*

6. *Assign one person to guard the permission base.*
7. *Work to decrease your cost of frequency by automating responses and moving to email and the internet.*
8. *Rebuild your website to turn it from brochureware* (infrequently updated content) *to a focused permission acquisition medium.*
9. *Regularly audit your permission base to determine how deep your permission really is.*
10. *Leverage your permission by offering additional products or services or by co-marketing with partners.*

Enchantment is a book written by Guy Kawasaki. One must understand what people are thinking, feeling and believing to enchant them. Pursue your passions, because passionate people are enchanting. Find shared interests with other people to enchant them. Think of how you can help people when you meet them. Great enchanters are likeable and trustworthy.

Describe your business in 10 words that are short, clear, different and humble. Create a smooth path for people to succeed. Stay positive and don't scare them. Try to find ways to get people to imagine what you are going to do for them. Show people using your product or service and other people will want to use it too. Tell stories. Find something that you both agree on.

Don't attack your competition. It's silly.

1. Know your competition. Try their products. Talk to their customers.
2. Analyze the competition. What can we both do? What can each do or not do?
3. Frame your competition. When questioned about Apple's role as moral police for the App store, Steve Jobs of Apple said about Google, "Folks who want porn can buy an android phone." Stay positive on their product.

Create inspiring and entertaining content to enchant your relationships. Leave positive comments when you read something that you like. Shine a light on others and you will get noticed.

Sell your dream. Think of it as a screenplay and not a speech.

Act 1: Set up the story.

Act 2: Present the drama of what it could be.

Act 3: Resolve the story and explain how it might happen.

Post links on social media that point people to stories, videos and pictures they might not find without you. Use www.stumbleupon.com to find interesting links. Respond to your fans' posts promptly and personally.

In Sandi Krakowski's book, *Social Media the Fun Way!,* she explains how to create interest in a friendly manner. A major mistake in social media is bringing your drama there. Stay positive. Tell people that there's nothing that they can't do and encourage them to give themselves dreams.

Don't post too often on your social media platforms. Try to post a couple of times a day. Posting 10-15 minutes in the early morning, in the early afternoon and at night would be plenty.

The most important aspects of your activities on social media are your relationships, your engagements, listening and interacting.

Likeable Social Media is a book written by Dave Kerpen. He will show you how to delight your customers, create an irresistible brand, and be generally amazing on Facebook and other social networks.

Many businesses are marketing to increase their Facebook likes to their fan page. Do you understand the importance of this? Everything that you post automatically gets sent to your friends that have liked you on Facebook. Many times this message will also get sent to email if the friend that liked you receives email notification of postings. Your fan page is like a landing page for a website. Therefore your new content posted on your fan page can become instant marketing messages to your friends that already know, like and trust you.

Why should people "like" you on Facebook? I know that you have seen ads that say, *Like us on Facebook.* Most people will think WIIFM (What's in it for me?). You have to give them a reason to like you on Facebook or many people will not do it.

CoTweet and ExactTarget conducted a study on the Top Ten reasons consumers "like" fan pages on Facebook. Here they are:

1. To receive discounts and promos.
2. To show support for brands to friends.
3. To get a "freebie" (samples, coupons).
4. To stay informed about company activities.
5. For updates on future projects.
6. For updates on upcoming sales.
7. Just for fun.
8. To get access to exclusive content.
9. To learn more about the company.
10. For education about company topics.

Say *Thank You* when they like your fan page. Thanks Man - You Rule! You Rock, Bro! You go, Girl!

I have been using Constant Contact for about a year to share information with employees. Several months ago, I received a gift in the mail from them. It was a book called *Engagement Marketing, How Small Business Wins in a Socially Connected World* written by their CEO, Gail F. Goodman. There is some great information in this book to help your small business grow.

Use technology to create a community where customers feel they are part of your business. Seasonal planting tips, event notices and weather alerts are some ideas to use. Respond whenever you are mentioned. Use hashtags in Twitter for your events or exhibitions to solicit discussion from your followers.

Make your customers the star of the show by using their pictures. Ask them if you can interview them for your Facebook, blog or newsletter. Get check-ins at your business through Facebook or Foursquare, a location-based social networking website for mobile devices, such as smartphones. Create a platform for specific content that your customers will want to add to and use. Avoid overloading your friends, connections or followers by posting excessively. The more visual and engaging your posts are, the more times they will be shared in social media. Consistently spend time on social media. Share articles that you find and give your commentary. Try pictures of direct mail pieces as content to share. Show screenshots of websites as content to share. Provide a Wow experience at your business, stay in touch and engage people.

Facebook, Twitter and Foursquare have many amazing ways to help you successfully market your business. However, the main focus of these powerhouse social media platforms is *personal*. The major focus of people that get involved in LinkedIn is *business*.

Wayne Breitbarth has given us insight on how to kick-start your business, brand and job search in his book, *The Power Formula for LinkedIn Success.*

LinkedIn is an online resume on steroids. Strategically fill out your profile with key words of importance. This will help your connections find you when searching for a product or service that you have to offer.

There are many built-in applications to facilitate sharing of your activities like posting a review of a book you read, a slide-share that you created, PDFs of helpful information about your business, upcoming events and You Tube video collections.

Get involved in LinkedIn business groups and share your insights. This is a great way to meet people. Think of these groups as an online networking meeting.

BUSINESS SECRET #14

BROKEN WINDOWS - BROKEN BUSINESS

Broken Windows, Broken Business is a book written by Michael Levine. This book shows how the smallest remedies can reap the biggest rewards in your business. The main idea is that when you make sure that your business is free of broken, scratched or worn parts, your business will grow without the help of any advertising.

Levine talks about large corporations, such as Kmart and Enron, who held the ideology that their businesses were strong, no matter how many broken windows they had. They were wrong.

Then he shared the story about a dentist that had been in business for many years, but his annual revenue was consistently dropping. He hired a business consultant who inspected the business. He felt the dentist and his staff did a great job for the customers, but the overall appearance of the office was old and worn. The suggestion was to repaint and modernize the entire office. The dentist liked the idea. They put up pictures of people smiling with pearly-white teeth all around the public walls. In the waiting area, he installed a plasma television showing testimonials of happy patients.

What was the result of these activities? Remember, there was no advertising. The first year sales rose 30%, and by the second year, he saw a 50% rise in business. What a difference! His return on the remodeling investment was more than positive. Think of how you can apply this to your business.

I have done my own research of businesses in Las Vegas. What I found was that maintenance problems were scarce in extremely busy offices and that maintenance problems were easy to find in businesses that were slow. I did this research recently, in the last several years when the Las Vegas economy was certainly much slower that it had been in earlier years.

After I read this book, I decided to look at my own business. It was worn too. I then upgraded and repainted it. I didn't see the profits the dentist had, but it certainly increased my bottom line.

What do your customers expect from you when they purchase your products or services? Are you giving them that, plus a little more? You should know what they expect and give that "little more" to them if you expect to grow, be successful and profit. Ask yourself these questions about expectations and reality:

1. What does my customer have a right to expect when he or she contacts my business?
2. Am I currently providing what my customer should logically expect?
3. Are my employees providing that extra something, even the ones who don't come in contact with the public?
4. Are there ways I can exceed my customer's expectations for my business?
5. How can I implement these "above and beyond" provisions and remain profitable?
6. Are my employees motivated to find ways to exceed our customer's expectations? Am I encouraging them to do so?
7. What should I do to go beyond the norm and make my business stand out in the customer service area?

The Broken Windows for Business Pledge

I _____, having read the concepts of the broken windows for business theory, do hereby pledge to do the following:

- I will pay attention to every detail of my business, especially those that seem insignificant.

- I will correct any broken windows I find in my business, and I will do so immediately, with no hesitation.
- I will screen, hire, train, and supervise my employees to notice and correct broken windows in the least amount of time possible.
- I will treat each customer like the only customer my business has.
- I will be on a constant vigil for signs of Broken Windows and will be sure never to assume my business is invulnerable.
- I will mystery shop my own business to discover broken windows that I hadn't noticed before.
- I will make sure every customer who encounters my business is met with courtesy, efficiency, and a smile.
- I will exceed my customer's expectations.
- I will be sure to always make a positive first impression and will assume that every impression is a first impression.
- I will make sure that my online and telephone customer service representatives do everything possible to solve a customer's problem *perfectly* the first time.
- I will be obsessive and compulsive when it comes to my business.

Signed this _____ day of _____,

in the year _____, by

_____

BUSINESS SECRET #15

FIVE WAYS TO MASSIVE PROFITS

I learned about the five ways to massive profits from Nate Smith of ActionCOACH. The compounding of these five ways can increase your business profits by 61% by increasing each of the five ways by only 10%. Thinking that you need increased business profits alone just won't work. By focusing on each of these five ways to be more efficient – individually rather than collectively – it's easier to accomplish and a more effective way to increase the profits of your business.

The Five Ways are:

1. ***Leads*** - The total number of people who your business has contacted, or have contacted your business over a period of time.
2. ***Conversion Rate*** - The percentage of people who actually make a purchase compared to your total number of leads. If you had 100 leads and 20 of those leads

bought from you, 20% would be your conversion rate.
3. *Average Sale Value* - The average amount that each business customer will buy from you on each visit. If your sales for the last 90 days were $100,000 and there were 1,000 different times that a customer came into your store and bought from you, your average sale value would be $100.
4. *Number of Transactions* - The average number of times that the same customer will come in and purchase during a period of time. This can be an estimate if you're not yet tracking this type of information at your business.
5. *Profit Margin* - The average profit percentage on each sale. If your total sales for the last 90 days was $100,000 and your total cost of buying your products and all other costs for the same period was $90,000, your profit would be $10,000. Your Profit Margin would then be calculated by dividing $10,000 into $100,000. The result would be 10%.

Here is an example of how increasing each of the five ways by 10% would increase profits by 61% or $488.

Name	Before 10% Increase	After 10% Increase
Leads	200	220
Conversion Rate	20%	22%
Total Customers	40	48.4
Transaction	2	2.2
Avg. Sale Value	$20	$22
Total Revenue	$1,600.00	$2,342.60
Profit Margin	50%	55%
Total Profits	**$800.00**	**$1,288.40**

Isn't it amazing that just a few small changes can make such a big difference in the total profits of your business?

You can download ActionCOACH's five-way calculator application to your Apple phone. It makes it real easy to visualize how much of a difference these five ways can add to your business' total profit. The application explains each way to you and gives examples on how to increase each one.

Here are five of the 75 strategies listed on the App to increase *lead generation*:

1. Direct mail
2. Radio advertising
3. Daily newspaper advertising

4. Internet and web pages
5. Cold calling

Here are five of the 84 strategies to increase *conversion rates:*

1. Written guarantee
2. Use a testimonial list
3. On-Hold messages
4. Take credit cards, checks and EFT
5. Audio, video and CD sale demos

Here are five of the 53 strategies to increase *average sale value:*

1. Stop discounting
2. Educate on value and not price
3. Increase your prices
4. Up sell
5. Use a questionnaire

Here are five of the 67 strategies listed to increase *number of transactions:*

1. Better service. Make your customers feel special, give them magic moments.
2. Under promise and over deliver.
3. Keep in regular contact with your customers.
4. Re-book customer's next visit now.
5. Build relationships with your customers.

Here are five of the 66 strategies listed to increase p*rofit margin:*

1. Set monthly expenditure budgets.
2. Reduce all of your costs.
3. Only sell fast-moving stock.
4. Buy in bulk to buy at lower prices.
5. Invest in technology.

To be able to have the five ways help your business increase profits, your business needs to track all of the actual statistics. Take the time and do the work yourself or hire it out. Find a computer program that will give you this information, or alter/add this to your existing program. This formula *and* implementing strategies to increase the five ways is your secret to success in your business.

BUSINESS SECRET #16

CUSTOMER OR CLIENT LISTS

What do you think is the most valuable asset in your business? Could it be your physical building? Could it be your equipment? Could it be your team members? Could it be your product? Could it be your specific service process? Could it be your location? Could it be the cash in your bank account? Could it be your marketing plan? Could it be your documented business systems?

You might think it might be one of the above assets or maybe all of these assets combined. These are all important assets to have, but none of them are the most important asset to your business.

The most important asset to your business is your Customer or Client Lists.

Why would I say this? You might not have guessed it. That's okay, because most business owners don't worry about maintaining such a list. But those same business owners are either failing or not living up to the real potential of their business.

Think about this. How busy are you? Does your customer have many distractions in their lives? I know that I sure have a lot of distractions in my life. I've bought a product or service from a local business and thought how glad I found them and certainly planned on going back. I was planning to go back next week, then it was next month, and then I realized it was six months and I still hadn't gone back there.

Then I noticed that business was closed. Why would such a wonderful business like that go out of business? One reason was that I hadn't gone back there. How many other people had not gone back even though they really liked this business?

Imagine if I and others that liked this business had been reminded in some fashion about this business. We probably would have gone back. This business would most likely still be there, and growing.

Many businesses will spend money on advertising and not make sure that they acquire their new customer's contact information. It's very hard to actually make an overall profit by spending advertising money to get a customer in only once.

Let's look at the numbers. How about spending $500 on distributing flyers for a pizza shop? Then let's say that 20 people show up from the flyer. Let's also say that the average sale of these customers was $25 and that their cost of sales was $10. For this example we won't consider extra wear and tear on the business or that maybe the business spent on extra man hours because of the advertising investment.

By getting the 20 new customers in only once, the pizza shop ended up spending $25 per customer in advertising dollars (20 x $25 = $500). Factoring in that the cost of sales was $10, this pizza shop lost $10 per customer x 20 customers or $200. This was not a good return on investment of the pizza shop's advertising dollars.

Now let's say that all of these customers really liked your food and said they wanted to come back. You acquired their contact information. You sent them an irresistible offer once a month for a year and on average, 80% of these new customers came back and bought $25 each time. Let's also say that it cost $1 to send each irresistible offer to these customers each month, or $20 a month.

What would be the profit now?

If 80% of those 20 new customers returned, that would equal 16 returning monthly customers. 16 customers x 12 returning visits for purchase would be 192 visits for the year. 192 visits times the gross profit per visit of $15 would be $2,880. It cost $20 x 12 to send the irresistible offer, or $240. Your net profit would now be $2,640 on this advertising activity. Your return on advertising investment would now have a 12 to 1 ratio.

WOW!

Does it now seem like the customer or client list is the most important asset in your business?

What type of information should you get from your new and existing customers or clients?

Here is a good list of customer information to get:

- Customer name
- Spouse name
- Address
- Text phone
- Email address
- Social media name
- Birthday of customer
- Birthday of spouse
- Anniversary date

Guard the safety of your customer list like it's money in your pocket, because it is. It's your future.

When you go to sell your business, it will be much more valuable when you have a detailed customer list. Keep track of their information when the customer shows up. Send them Thank You cards for coming in. If you can, find out what personal interests that they have, and be sure to note it in your database.

BUSINESS SECRET #17

COACHES, CONSULTANTS AND MENTORS

Today's world seems to appreciate self-made athletes, millionaires, musicians, authors and just about any other category that you could become famous for. Do you really think that they or you will accomplish your lofty goals all by yourself? Many people do. Can you really teach yourself everything that you need to know to run your business successfully? How much will it cost you to make those mistakes? How much did you not earn during the time you were making those mistakes?

Michael Jordan, one of the best NBA basketball players of all time, had a coach. The main reason Michael Jordan retired was that his coach who had been with him his entire career decided to retire.

"Everyone needs a coach," Eric Schmidt said in an interview, who is the founder and CEO of Google.com. "Every famous athlete, every famous performer has somebody who has had a coach. Somebody who can watch what they're doing and say, "Is that what you really meant? Did you really do that?" They can give them perspective. The one thing people are never good at is seeing themselves as others see them. A coach really, really helps."

What is a coach? A coach is someone who will help lead you to accomplish the goals that you have without doing any of the actual work. They may help a little in doing the actual work, but not much. They will critique your progress to help you successfully accomplish your goals.

What is a consultant? A consultant will help in leading you towards your goals, but does more of the actual work. They may create documents, videos or audios. They are involved in the creation of the actual procedures that are necessary for you to accomplish your goals. They will also critique your progress to help you successfully accomplish your goals.

What is a mentor? A mentor is usually a friend or acquaintance that will help point you in the right direction. You usually will receive small pieces of great information on how you will accomplish your goals in small segments of time.

Over the years I have had music teachers to help me learn how to excel at the Clarinet, Saxophone, Flute, Guitar, Piano and Vocals. I enjoyed learning from books and videos. I practiced many hours on my own. When I picked up bad habits, my teachers would help lead me away from those into much more successful playing than I could ever have done on my own.

I ran for office in Las Vegas five times and unfortunately, I lost each and every time. I was always looking for help, but help was hard to find. I studied everything that I could get my hands on in regards to winning the election. Each time I lost, I studied more and tried to figure out how I could better myself. My friend, Bob Beers, mentored me numerous times on how to become a better candidate. Without his help, I would not have become as good as a candidate as I was. My friend and mentor, Elmer Chowning, convinced me that getting elected was more about representing the power of money and influential groups than it was about representing the needs of the people. That was the reason I lost and why I am no longer voting or running for office.

My point is? They were all coaches that I needed throughout my entire life.

I am not completely focusing on running and creating successful businesses. I received some great marketing coaching help from Richelle Shaw, who also authored the book, *How to Build a Million Dollar Business in Las Vegas.*

I received some great overall business coaching help from Nate Smith of ActionCOACH, and now I'm working on increasing my social media awareness and writing with the help of Nina Lewis. She is an amazing lady that is helping me brainstorm how I want to accomplish getting the word out to business owners in Las Vegas.

I have an incredible sales coach in Stevenson Brooks. I searched for sales coaching in Las Vegas and interviewed a few of them. He told me about David Sandler's book, *You Can't Teach a Kid to Ride a Bike at a Seminar: The Sandler Sales Institute's 7-Step System for Successful Selling* and his other sales books. I hired him to help me and he has great insight in the sales process that has been invaluable to my success.

I have also invested a lot of time in creating documents, flyers, newsletters, and websites through the use of Microsoft Word and Publisher and my website program called Hubspot.

I learned a very important lesson recently in regards to creating marketing pieces on my own. A marketing consultant helping me at Larry's Hideaway used his own professional graphic artist to help promote getting new customers in the door. The results he created in a short period of time were amazing. I have since hired a professional graphic artist to help me create new marketing pieces for BHI Bookkeeping. When you look more professional, you sell more. Invest the money on professional writers and graphic artists.

Nineteen years ago I hired New Clients Inc. by going to a seminar and by having ongoing phone support. They really acted as consultants that had developed an effective marketing system for accountants like me. They helped to grow my bookkeeping business then and continue to do so today. The economy and other challenges that have hit my business hard which led me to going back to them for a refresher course last month.

I also had numerous other coaches and consultants to help. Consider investing in this kind of help for your business.

Hire professionals to help you and watch how amazing results start to roll in.

BUSINESS SECRET #18

ONE SMALL NICHE BUSINESS

To be the leader of a small business, you need to be confident that you can do just about everything because you probably will have to. After you realize that you can do so many things well, you might think that you could also broaden your horizons and open and run other businesses. Let me caution you: very few of us can run numerous different types of businesses at the same time successfully and profitably.

It's much wiser to run one type of business and be able to create and implement marketing, manage the operations, and maintain accurate and timely accounting records successfully. If your business is running smoothly, profitably and growing, consider opening another location. Create effective plans for growth and implement them.

If you are personally interested in other types of business, sell the business you have and go into the next business with 100% of your efforts.

I have learned this from my own experiences of juggling numerous businesses at the same time. When I started BHI in 1978, I did most everything myself until 1993, when I started marketing and growing. When I focused fully on its operation, it grew to a business of $1,000,000 in annual sales.

With five years experience as a Nevada Worker's Compensation auditor, I decided to get my insurance license to represent my clients when Nevada changed their monopolistic laws in regards to workers comp in 1999. I did pretty well with it financially. It was a time-eater though and I didn't like this type of business because of all of the regulations put upon agents. It took away from my existing business too. I asked Chrystal if she would like to run this business for me. My oldest daughter has run it ever since and does a great job.

Several years later I thought to add the ability to sell mutual funds to my clients. I passed all of the tests and found that I really did not like this type of business and turned off all of my licenses. This time took away from my profitable bookkeeping business.

These were three distinct types of businesses. Even though they were completely involved in making sure the overall accounting systems of my clients were maintained accurately and timely, they were still separate niches. If I had limited myself to one of the parts, I would have succeeded much more. Hindsight is always 20/20!

In 2006, a client of mine for about 20 years passed away and his trust was placed into my hands. He had three operating businesses named Rancho True Value hardware store, Larry's Hideaway and Larry's Villa. I was granted a gaming, liquor, topless and hardware license to operate them. Along with BHI and its insurance division, I managed these other businesses as well.

I overloaded myself with responsibilities. I had given it huge effort, but managing all of these businesses at the same time was not successful. I tried delegating many duties to different managers, but I didn't know enough yet how to create and maintain proper business systems to effectively handle all of these responsibilities.

Rancho True Value Hardware store was up against Lowes and Home Depot. I created a small niche where we could compete. That niche was to be the best at paint and plumbing in the valley. I hired a new manager named John and asked him to manage the changeover in the business model. He worked hard and made changes very quickly. We had the most types of paint and paint vendors in the Las Vegas Valley. The plumbing side did not fare so well. The problem was, the Las Vegas economy was shrinking at the same time we'd started the new model. Within nine months, it was obvious that we could not make it and I sold it to Ahern Rentals for a good price.

The concept was good, but you cannot delegate passion for success. You cannot just hire out the creation of a new business by having the manager do everything. John worked long hours, but I couldn't focus on this business because I had four others to take care of.

But now I could invest time into Larry's Hideaway, a country dance hall with gaming and liquor sales. It was named *hideaway* because its location was set off of a main highway called Rancho Drive. I was fully involved with marketing and management. I learned how to country two-step and line dance very well! I also learned many things related to country music. I learned about the type of customers that came in and how competition affected our success. I even created a band to play country dancing music that I chipped in as bass player to help. I never found the magic bullet to make it a financial success and on June 30, 2012, I closed Larry's Hideaway and put it up for sale.

Larry's Villa is being administered by hiring managers that report to me. Mostly it has been profitable, but it has yet to meet its full potential

Managing all of these businesses at once has taken its toll on me personally and all of my business ventures. I have shared these stories to help you learn to stay in one business and do it very well. Find a small niche that you can be known as the best of the best.

BUSINESS SECRET #19

SELL ON VALUE - DON'T SELL ON PRICE

Most confident business owners think that if they can just get customers in the door, they will buy. But what offer will get them in the door? Many business owners offer discounts to entice their customers to come in. They figure that if they can get the customer to buy once at a discount, they'll just keep coming back to buy more at regular price.

What customers do you really want for your business? What is the target market of your business? Why is this important to the success of your business? It is important to the future profitability of your business. If you get the *correct* customers, your business will be more profitable.

New or continuing customers that come in and buy on price are a specific targeted market. These customers will go to businesses that offer the best discount normally and will probably not be loyal customers at your regular full price.

I learned about this problem while promoting Larry's Hideaway for 6½ years. We could barely be seen off of Rancho Road, so we didn't get drive-by traffic. We used live bands as a customer draw, but bands cost a lot. Live bands brought in some customers and sent other customers away. Larry's Hideaway was an 8,000 square foot building with a huge dance floor, so it took a lot of customers to make it look like a fun place to be. Fifty customers in the bar looked empty, while 100 customers looked like it might start getting fun.

We needed more customers. We changed from the live band format to having our own country disc jockeys. We started promoting ladies night on Fridays, where ladies drinks cost $1 each. Of course, the idea was that when the ladies came, the men would come too. This idea worked very well to bring in new customers and keep customers coming back. We had customer counts of over 600 people on Friday nights on many occasions.

The problem came with the increased costs of security and costs of operation. Building repair costs shot up because of the sheer volume of people using the facilities. Ladies would give their $1 drinks to their male friends that would cut into our profit margin. Many nights we would lose money having 600+ people in the building!

Larry's Hideaway was 20 years and situated in a neighborhood. We had several competitors open up with new country dance halls inside casinos and on the Las Vegas strip.

One thing we couldn't do with Larry's Hideaway was pick it up and move it.

Even though customers enjoyed Larry's Hideaway, they started going to the new competitors like Stoneys, Revolver and Gilly's. They paid more for their drinks there and also had to pay a cover charge.

We lost those customers because these new competitors offered a better value than Larry's Hideaway. They were novel, had high ceilings, visibility from walking by a casino or drive-by traffic, large advertising budgets to remind customers to come, top well-known country bands to attract them, large video screens and many other extra values. Customers that had been coming to Larry's Hideaway were now going to the new competition, stating that it was just more fun for them.

You can't just build your business on the lowest cost. You need to build value into the product or service that you sell so that there is no competition on price.

Take gas stations, for example. The only one that ever wins in a price war of gas stations that are across the street from each other is the customers themselves.

Customers buy when the cost of their purchase is less than their perceived value of their purchase. Find ways to build value into your product or service that adds value without adding much cost. This will help your customers buy from you more often. This will also differentiate you from the competition, so that you're not competing in a price war.

BUSINESS SECRET #20

U.S.P. – UNIQUE SELLING PROPOSITION

Dan S. Kennedy's book, *No B.S. Price Strategy, The Ultimate No Holds Barred, Kick Butt, Take No Prisoners Guide to Profits, Power and Prosperity*, can help you further understand selling on value.

A Unique Selling Proposition is formed by having your business complete answers to the following two questions:

1. Why should I, your prospect, choose to do business with you vs. any and every other option available?
2. Why should I, your prospect, choose you regardless of price, be unconcerned about price, and never consider comparison shopping based on price?

You should use these answers in your primary sales message to your prospects.

U.V.P. or Unique Value Proposition is where you find ways to make price a non-issue or to make the product pay for itself. You might do this by bundling services together at a lower price than purchased separately. You want to show that the values of your products or services are far in excess of the price. You might show that your product pays for itself such as in the example of buying energy efficient windows that pay for themselves through lower power bills.

U.S.P. or Unique Safety Proposition revolves around a guarantee or risk reversal. This is also where you would reassure your prospects that your product is safe for them to buy using testimonials, client lists, years in business or number of clients that have bought your service.

Extraordinary Guarantees, Achieving Breakthrough Gains in Quality and Customer Satisfaction written by Christopher W. Hart, Ph.D. will help you fully understand the magic of an Extraordinary Guarantee. As a business-building program, the 100% Satisfaction Guarantee has been an overwhelming success. Here are the benefits of a 100% Satisfaction Guarantee:

- Unifies organizational commitment to guest satisfaction.
- Focuses organization on guests' perceptions of product and service.

- Empowers employees and motivates them to deliver excellent product and service.
- Reduces employee turnover.
- Attracts new guests.
- Increases positive word-of-mouth.
- Acts as an insurance policy that increases guest retention.
- Uncovers opportunities for service improvement.
- Assures consistent high-quality service delivery.
- Improves financial performance.

U.E.P. or Unique Experience Proposition is where people most willingly buy and pay premiums for complete, total, enjoyable, and unusual experiences. This is where the future of selling your products or services is going. The idea is not to put the primary emphasis on your products or service, but to put the main emphasis on the experience of using, buying or enjoying your product or service.

Irresistible Offer is another component of your business's successful Unique Selling Proposition. Mark Joyner in his book, *The Irresistible Offer: How to Sell Your Product or Service in 3 Seconds or Less*, helps us further understand the irresistible offer.

Here is one quote from his book:

"Each advertisement must make a proposition to the consumer. Not just words, not just product puffery, not just show-window advertising. Each advertisement must say to each reader: Buy this product and you will get this specific benefit. The proposition must be one that the competition either cannot, or does not, offer. It must be unique – either a uniqueness of the brand or a claim not otherwise made in that particular field of advertising."

These are some examples of Irresistible Offers:

- *"Be All You Can Be" – "An Army of One"* – U.S. Army
- *"You Give Us 22 Minutes. We'll Give You The World"* – WINS Radio in New York
- *"We'll Beat Anyone's Advertised Price or your Mattress is Freeeeee!"* – Sit 'n Sleep
- *"48-Hour Parts Service Anywhere in the World or Caterpillar Pays"* – Caterpillar Tractor
- *"Ten Years Trouble-Free Operation"* – Maytag
- *"If You're Not Satisfied for Any Reason, We'll Take it Back Without a Receipt" – No Questions Asked"* – Nordstrom's Department Stores
- *"The 100 Percent Solution"* – Re/Max real estate

- *"Before and After"* – Merle Norman Cosmetics
- *"Free Samples"* – Mrs. Fields Cookies

The Benefit of the Benefit is another component of the Unique Selling Proposition. The Benefit of the Benefit is fully explained in Steve Bryant's book, *Sales Magic: Increase your sales dramatically. Proven techniques by one of America's top sales and marketing experts.*

When you are going through your sales presentation, you will normally go through three distinct sections. They are called the features of your product or service, the advantages of your product or service, and the benefit to your prospect of your product or service. There is a fourth section that most sales presentations omit. That is the benefit of the benefit, or what product or service really means to your prospect. I will give you an example so that you will fully understand the four parts and the benefit of the benefit.

New state-of-the-art copier system:

1. **Features:** (Introduce Product – This is _____) – A copier creates exact duplicates of documents.
2. **Advantages:** (Describe Product – Which Does _____) – These copies improve

3. both inter- and intra-company communication.
4. **Benefit to Prospect:** (How will it help customer? – Which Means _____) – This improved communication will allow the company to grow at a greater rate, improving its bottom line. These better communications would make the company more competitive, a very important point in tough economic times.
5. **Benefit of the Benefit:** (Individual Effect on Customer after getting the benefit – Which means _____ to my customer) – This company could use this copier to create newsletters to keep in touch with the customers in an effort to keep them as customers longer, have them buy more and get more referrals. That will increase profits and cash flow to the business owner. This in turn will decrease stress to the owner… and the personal Benefit of the Benefit will be:

More Time and More Smiles.

Another very helpful book from Sandler Training written by David Mattson and Anthony Parinello is *Five Minutes with VITO: Making the most of your selling time with the Very Important Top Officer.* This book helps us understand that we need to get our idea through to buyers quickly because most lose interest very quickly. It points out that your business needs Hard Value and Soft Value delivered to its customers. Here are explanations and examples of Hard Value and Soft Value:

Hard Value: (THE MEASURABLE BENEFIT TO MY VIP CUSTOMER WAS THAT WE ....) *Improved efficiency of knowledge based workers by up to 2.8% ...*

(AND WE DID THIS BY MEANS OF A UNIQUE PROCESS THAT ALLOWED THEM TO ...) *get those knowledge workers spending more time analyzing and making decisions and less time gathering the information necessary to facilitate those decisions.*

Soft Value: (THE UNMEASURABLE BENEFIT TO MY VIP CUSTOMER WAS THAT WE ....) *protected valuable market share and sustained their competitive edge...*

(AND WE DELIVERED THIS BY MEANS OF A UNIQUE PROCESS THAT ALLOWED THEM TO ...) *proactively identify and respond to competitor price moves and promotional offers – without lowering price points.*

These are just some of the ideas to help you create an effective Unique Selling Proposition that will get your prospects to buy now and more often. This will increase your bottom line profits and increase cash in your bank account. Get started creating your Unique Selling Proposition today.

BUSINESS SECRET #22

STRATEGIZE YOUR BUSINESS FOR GENERATION Y

Generation Y people were born between 1978 and 2000. They are now 11 to 32 years old and revolutionizing retail. Your business needs to speak to them in their language and where they are or your business will get left behind.

Kit Yarrow, Ph.D. and Jayne O'Donnell can help you better understand how your business should relate to Generation Y better in their book *Gen BuY: How Tweens, Teens, and Twenty-Somethings are Revolutionizing Retail.*

Gen Y accounts for 37% of all money spent in the United States. Currently they are 26% of the population or 84 million people, but by 2015 they will be 34% of the population. Baby Boomers account for currently 78 million people as of the 2009 writing of this book. They have powerful influence on their parents. Think about it. Do you ask your children for advice? I ask my daughters for advice all the time and they have an amazing and powerful point of view.

Resource Interactive Study done in the fall of 2007 shows how much influence Gen Y has on household purchases in the following categories: 90% on Clothing - 85% on Videos - 85% on Groceries - 77% on Video Games - 71% on Cell Phones - 67% on Sports Equipment - 65% on Vacations and 49% on Vehicles.

Technology is currency to them. They want it now. They want great service and perfection. Gen Y is the most educated, affluent, diverse population ever in the history of the United States. Combine that with hip environment, instant gratification, must be fashionable, fusion of virtual and real, interactive, visual, emotional, and the need for humanized company that connects with them in a genuine and emphatic way. Personalized communication is the avenue that they want. They need information more quickly and more stimuli. Their tolerance for Boredom is low. Mix in vivid colors, creative design and sensual lighting.

A whopping 65% of Gen Y learns about products on the net. Of teens, 75% enjoy figuring out how to make devices work. They spend most of their time on social media and use friends on Facebook for name dropping. Most (75%) view their computer more for entertainment than TV. Sixty-percent of 18 - 24 year olds view gift cards as the best gift. Two-thirds love to shop and most view shopping as a stress reliever. They use shopping as a way to prepare emotionally for events. They become overly dependent on shopping. Most (75%) of ages 24- 32 prefer email. They spend as much time talking as texting about purchases.

Gen Y is less about quantity of product and more about the experience. That could explain why the next economy is expected to be the *experience* economy. Find ways to be interactive with them. Make sure your business is noticed in places where *they* are such as on cell phones, computers, at school or at the movies. Create a community for Generation Y to talk to themselves and your business. Get close to them. Understand why they have the opinions that they have and why they do what they do. Be in their shoes. Engage and inspire them. They want to be part of your business process from design to delivery. They admire strength but not power. They also admire humanness, humor and inspiration.

Make them feel like they are saving and not spending. Prime the sales pump. The first dollar is hard to get from them, but the second dollar is much easier. They are less likely to have a mortgage and kids than earlier generations. They have an ongoing struggle with debt management because they most likely had everything as kids.

The majority of Generation Y love to play video games. Remember also that pictures really need to say it all to them and those great pictures about your product are more important than ever before.

BUSINESS SECRET #22

ANCIENT SECRETS TO WEALTH

George S. Clason wrote the most inspiring book on wealth ever written called *The Richest Man in Babylon.* It is written in old English, so I decided to share with you its secrets in the language it was written in. Since 1926, it has sold over 2 million copies and is as important to you and your business today and in the future as it ever was in the time of Babylon. Use these secrets and they should help you become wealthy. Here are the secrets:

Lo, Money is Plentiful for those who Understand the Simple Rules of Acquisition

1. Start thy purse to fattening .
2. Control thy expenditures.
3. Make thy Gold Multiply.
4. Guard thy Treasures from Loss.
5. Make thy Dwelling a Profitable Investment.

6. Insure thy Future Income.
7. Increase thy Ability to Earn.

The Five Laws of Gold

1. Gold cometh gladly and in increasing quantity to any man who will put by not less than one-tenth of his earnings to create an estate for his future and that of his family.

2. Gold laboreth diligently and contentedly for the wise owner who finds for it profitable employment, multiplying even as the flocks of the field.

3. Gold clingeth to the protection of the cautious owner who invests it under the advice of men wise in its handling.

4. Gold slippeth away from the man who invests it in businesses or purposes with which he is not familiar or which are not approved by those skilled in its keep.

5. Gold flees the man who would force it to impossible earnings or who followeth the alluring advice of tricksters and schemers or who trust it to his own inexperience and romantic desires in investment.

Where the Determination is, the Way can be Found.

Men of Action are Favored by the Goddess of Good Luck.

BUSINESS SECRET #23

8 WAYS TO GREAT

8 Ways to Great: Peak Performance on the Job and in Your Life is a book written by Dr. Doug Hirschhorn who delivers an exceptional, no-frills guide to tapping into and maximizing your inner strengths.

Here are some great questions to ask yourself:

- Why are you doing what you do?
- Why are you doing what you are doing for a living?
- Why did you originally choose what you are currently doing for a living?
- Why are you still doing what you are doing for a living?
- What do you really want to do with the rest of your life?
- What would you rather be doing?
- What are 3 to 5 of your strengths and weaknesses?

- How can your strengths help you become better?
- How can your strengths get in your way of being successful?
- What is your upside if you succeed?
- What is your downside if you fail?
- What is your net payoff for doing what you do for a living?
- What do you love, care about or value?

Spend some time thinking about these questions to really know about yourself and why you are doing what you do for a living. If you really don't know why you are doing it, you will never really be successful.

Here are the summarized principles of the 8 Ways to Great:

Principle #1: Find Your "Why" – Determine specifically what your core motivation is to do what you do for a living.

Principle #2: Get to Know Yourself – Really get to know your strengths and weakness and focus your energies on how and what you do things best.

Principle #3: Learn to Love the Process – Learn to enjoy working on the small steps that lead you towards your overall goal. The journey is always more important than the final destination.

Principle #4: Sharpen your Edge - Learn what sets you apart from your competition and get even better at it.

Principle #5: Be All That You Can Be – Judge yourself only in terms of your own abilities. Always strive for your personal best. Never compare yourself to how others do what you are doing.

Principle #6: Keep Your Cool – Don't be afraid of doing what you want to do. Don't be afraid of failing. Always understand that what you are doing is in the best interests of you and your business.

Principle #7: Get Comfortable with Being Uncomfortable: When you venture off in another direction from what you are currently doing, there will be many obstacles in your way. There are also many things that could go wrong. If you don't try, you will never succeed. Nothing with ever be perfect to start. Start now and adjust what you do with what you learn. Keep at it and you can be very successful.

Principle #8: Make Yourself Accountable – Unless there is some meaningful reward for performing well and an equally meaningful consequence for making a stupid mistake or breaking your own rules, you may not take the steps necessary to put your best-laid plans into action. Ask someone to help you hold yourself accountable if you don't think you can hold yourself accountable.

BUSINESS SECRET #24

HIRE SLOW, FIRE FAST

This has been a hard one for me, but I am getting better at it. I have been hiring employees, contractors and vendors for 32 years. Some that I have hired were mostly successful hires, however many more hires have been huge disappointments. I have always been in a position to need the help, so I would overlook the hire's shortcomings if they were getting most of what I needed accomplished. Or, I was just too busy to consider alternatives. This is certainly one of the most challenging problems to a growing business.

While BHI Bookkeeping was growing, I was always looking for new employees. Many times there were just not enough hours in the day. I decided to quicken the pace of hiring by putting up tests for possible hires on Craigslist. The prospect needed to follow all instructions in the ad or I would not even consider them. I felt as though if they could not follow instructions to get the job, why would the hiring prospect follow procedures after they got the job.

I remember one hire named Pete. He had great experience in bookkeeping and income tax preparation, seemed like he was comfortable with the pay rate and followed all of the instructions perfectly that I listed on my Craigslist ad. I called him on the phone while I was on vacation and hired him because I needed someone now. That was a mistake. Pete turned out to have a very strange personality that annoyed many of the clients. He continued to work for me for about five years, even though several clients quit over his personality. One day when a client fired him, I finally had fire him as well. His response was to collect unemployment compensation and go into the bookkeeping business for himself with six clients that he'd cultured.

The lesson that I learned from Pete was to make sure that I always met the possible new hire before I decided to hire him. I also learned that I should have fired him much quicker.

I had another employee, Bob, who worked for me about 14 years. He worked very hard delivering and picking up bookkeeping materials. It was a tough job and he was very efficient at it. The problem with Bob was that he could get very mad at the clients, fellow employees or me at any moment. He would always apologize for his actions. Then I would tell him to not ever do that again. In the last few years of his employment, we started losing clients over Bob's actions.

The lesson that I learned from Bob was that I should have fired him much quicker. I should *never* have lost clients from the actions of our delivery person. I left him employed because I was too busy and felt there just wasn't enough time to go through the rehiring process right then. I'm sure many small business owners have been in the same position.

I could go through many more examples of hiring and firing problems, but I would rather go into solutions.

ActionCOACH suggested that I read Geoff Smart and Randy Street's book, *Who: The A Method for Hiring*, to help me solve my hiring challenges.

When you hire, obviously you only want to hire A people for your position (as opposed to B, C or D people). You need to see pre-defined levels of success that the hired employee needs to accomplish. You also need to have pre-defined consequences for their inability to meet them. Follow through with your pre-defined consequences to that employee or no one else that works for you will believe that they really need to follow those success levels either.

Complete a scorecard for each new hire prospect on a scale of 1 to 10. Remember, you need to interview many people to increase your odds of hiring the right person for the right position. Include the following aspects of your new hire in your interview:

- How well will they fit into the chemistry that your team members already have?
- How committed will they be to the job?
- How coachable will they be?
- How under control is their Ego?
- How much of the required intellect do they have already to do the job?

Ask them questions like:

- What are your career goals?
- What are you really good at professionally?

Watch out for hiring prospects that:

- Want to win too much.
- Want to add too much value to your business.
- Seem like they would pass the buck.
- Excessively needs to be themselves.
- Uses *no*, *but* or *however* too much.
- Want to tell the world how smart they are.
- You hear them making too many excuses.

Create an A method of hiring your team members and an A method of managing your team members once you have them. Here are 10 ideas to help you create your best team:

1. Make team members your top priority.
2. Follow the same A methods yourself.
3. Build support for your systems among your team members.
4. Create a clear vision of your company and reinforce it through communication.
5. Train your team members on best practices of operating the business.
6. Remove barriers of success from your team members.
7. Implement new policies that support positive change.
8. Recognize and reward those that follow the systems you are implementing for the positive improvement of the business.
9. Remove managers that are not on board.
10. Celebrate the success that the business has achieved and plan for more change.

Follow these same procedures when you hire vendors, independent contractors or employees. There are huge costs associated with hiring incorrectly or continuing to work with ineffective team members inside or outside of your business.

BUSINESS SECRET #25

TEST TEAM MEMBERS BEFORE HIRING

I learned this the hard way when BHI was quickly growing and we always needed more help. Applicants would fill out an application, a simple questionnaire and I would interview them. If they sounded like they would be a good fit, I would try to hire them on the spot. I encountered many problems in the abilities of new team members with this simple system. Better information about the candidates was missed because I had not created good tests to get a better idea of the best team members for the job. Take the time to create the best tests for your new candidates in order to get the best team members for your vacant positions.

One type of test I recently discovered is called the D.I.S.C. personality test. This test helps you identify if your candidate has the best personality for the position you are considering them for. Each letter of D.I.S.C. stands for a different kind of personality. The results will usually be more prominent in one or two areas.

Here are explanations of each of the four different types of D.I.S.C. personalities:

D (Dominance): This personality type is independently minded and motivated to succeed. They are usually in positions of authority and rarely give up. You might think of them as CEOs. Only about 14% of the public would have this type of personality.

I (Influence): This personality type loves to communicate and is socially confident. They are usually impulsive and sometimes irrational. They don't really enjoy rejection. You might think of them in some type of sales position. About 32% of the public would have this type of personality.

S (Steadiness): This personality type is very patient and is also a sympathetic listener. They are interested in the problems and feelings of others. They enjoy support roles. You might think of them in customer support roles like human relations. About 27% of the public would have this type of personality.

C (Compliance): This personality type enjoys details and facts. The want precision and accuracy in their world. They usually have a lack of ambition and are unwilling to speak out. They love to control their environment as much as possible. You might think of them as accountants, engineers or critical thinkers. About 27% of the public would have this type of personality.

Make sure you match the correct personality of your new hire with the job that you are assigning them to.

Honesty is always critical to the success of any business. It is also a hard trait to test for. Even though I have yet to implement this next type of test in my business, I am strongly considering it. What other kind of action can you connect to lying or purposely misleading? The action I am talking about is drug abuse. You can test for it even though there are products available to create a false negative drug test. I have thought that what a team member does on their own time is their own concern and not that of the business. But lying and stealing affect the success of business.

So the real purpose of doing a drug test is not to catch a team member that does drugs. The real purpose of doing drug testing is getting rid of team members that most probably will lie or steal.

Create tests that will show whether the prospect for a new hire has the ability to do the job before you invest your money into finding out. Create a series of simple questions that anyone who works in your field would know easily. Create a simple math test, if math is needed in your field. Be creative. Figure out the reason that you had a bad hire before and add questions to your tests to have an opportunity to stop that same type of bad hire from happening again.

BUSINESS SECRET #26

BALANCE PERSONAL AND BUSINESS HAPPINESS TO GET THE MOST OUT OF YOUR LIFE

Do you spend a large portion of your day working in and on your business? Have you realized that you are working so hard on your business that it is having an effect on your relationships with your family, friends and spouse? Do you say to yourself that just as soon as I get over the latest big challenge at your business, that you will slow down and take time to enjoy your cherished relationships? Have you been neglecting your personal health by not eating right and not exercising because of all of the time you are investing to create your successful business?

Are you happy right now in your life?

Aristotle said, *"Happiness is the Meaning and Purpose of Life."* He certainly was not trying to point out if you work more, you will be happy.

Don't Sacrifice Money for Happiness!

Creating and operating a business can be very stressful. Remember that for you to be physically able to take on your business challenges, you need to be in top physical shape. Time that you spend exercising and focusing on eating right helps your business become more successful.

We all live in today. Enjoy every part of it. Sacrifice will not make you happy or pleasurable. Aristotle also quoted, *"Happiness Depends on Us."* Fill your life with as much happiness as possible, but don't expect constant happiness.

Tal Ben-Shahar, Ph.D. wrote a book to help you find happiness entitled, *Happier: Learn the Secrets to Daily Joy and Lasting Fulfillment.* To help yourself find happiness, ask yourself the following three questions:

1. What gives me meaning? In other words, what provides me with a sense of purpose?
2. What gives me pleasure? In other words, what do I enjoy doing?
3. What are my strengths? In other words, what am I good at?

Every day write five things that you are thankful for. Enjoy the journey and don't keep waiting for the future goal to be completed. You will just create another goal. Remember that happiness is involvement and progress towards your goals.

Another great quote by Aristotle is *"Without Friendships, No Happiness is Possible."*

Learn to say no. Ask yourself how you can simplify your life. Where can I cut? What can I give up?

Ben-Shahar put it all into one great statement about happiness. *"We are living a happy life when we derive pleasure and meaning while spending time with our loved ones, or learning something new or engaging in a project at work. The more days with these experiences the happier we become."*

When you are creating goals for yourself, create them for all aspects of your life. Don't just consider creating business goals.

Sometimes you need to find a little boost for happiness. *Zig Ziglar's Secrets of Closing the Sale* said to create a list of songs that will make you feel happy, so that you will be a better salesman. This book was written in 1984 and I adapted his idea for today. I searched in Google for happy and inspirational songs. I first listened to the songs in the iTunes store. I downloaded the ones I liked to my iPhone. Every morning I play the songs while getting ready for work. It puts me in a really happy mood to start the day. Try it. Here is the playlist I'm now using in alphabetical order:

1. *Chariots of Fire*, Starlight Orchestra
2. *Come on Over*, Shania Twain
3. *Easy*, The Commodores
4. *Eye of the Tiger*, Starlight Orchestra
5. *Good Vibrations*, The Beach Boys
6. *Heal the World*, Michael Jackson
7. *Hero*, Enrique Iglesias
8. *I Believe I Can Fly*, R. Kelly
9. *I Hope You Dance*, Lee Ann Womack
10. *I Will Always Love You*, Whitney Houston
11. *I Will Survive*, Gloria Gaynor
12. *I've Got the World on a String*, Frank Sinatra
13. *(I've Had) The Time of My Life*, Dirty Dancing
14. *If You're Going Through Hell*, Rodney Atkins
15. *It's a Great Day to Be Alive*, Travis Tritt
16. *Last Dollar (Fly Away)*, Tim McGraw
17. *Moondance*, Van Morrison
18. *My Way*, Frank Sinatra
19. *Never Surrender*, Corey Hart
20. *Reach*, Gloria Estefan
21. *Rocky*, Starlight Orchestra
22. *Singing in the Rain*, Gene Kelly
23. *Something More*, Sugarland

24. *Spooky*, Classics IV
25. *Stand*, Rascal Flatts
26. *That's What Friends Are For*, Dionne Warwick
27. *The Impossible Dream*, Luther Vandross
28. *Up*, Shania Twain
29. *Walking on Sunshine*, Katrina & the Waves
30. *What a Wonderful World*, Louis Armstrong
31. *When You Believe*, Mariah Carey
32. *Why Don't We Just Dance*, Josh Turner
33. *Win*, Brian McKnight
34. *Wonderful Tonight*, Eric Clapton
35. *Wouldn't It Be Nice*, Beach Boys
36. *You Are the Sunshine of My Life*, Stevie Wonder

BUSINESS SECRET #27

FULLY UNDERSTAND YOUR ACCOUNTING

What do I mean by fully understand your accounting? You might say that I have an accountant and he takes care of that so that I don't have to.

Willie Nelson hired one of the largest CPA firms in the world to take care of his taxes and blindly trusted how they prepared his tax return. The IRS audited him and ultimately bankrupted Willie. He did repay the taxes by creating a new album that earned enough money to repay the taxes. Now that was marketing genius!

Delegate and don't abdicate. Multiply your efforts by having others take care of duties for you, but diligently oversee that they were accomplished timely and accurately.

One of the ways that your business will continue to operate is if you make sure that all of your IRS and state tax reports are filed accurately, timely and paid in full. They have the power to shut down your business. Don't take this responsibility lightly.

Many business owners have told me that they knew they should be able to use their Profit and Loss statement as a tool for success in their business, but they didn't know how. They wished they could find a gentle accountant with real day-to-day business experience like themselves that understood them and didn't just tell them what to do or what they were doing wrong. Unfortunately, many business owners don't want to take a call from their accountant because that would just make them feel bad for not completing bookkeeping tasks they knew they should have done.

Other business owners have told me that they were embarrassed about their books and spent too much time doing their own bookkeeping. They worried that the work they did wasn't correct which could cause large IRS or state audits and penalties.

What is the answer then? The answer is to find the friendly and helpful forward-thinking profit and growth strategic partner for your business that will help you make sure your accounting systems are highly effective. The right person will be happy to educate you on how to oversee their efforts with your accounting system.

Work with your accountant to build your Profit and Loss statements in such a way that will help your business' effectiveness at producing profits. I worked with a client of mine that owned three Little Caesars' locations here in Las Vegas for many years. They were very profitable. One of the reasons was that he used his Profit and Loss statements as a tool to make sure his managers were effectively keeping costs down.

Little Caesars gave him the targeted cost percentage of each item on the menu when the franchisee followed the documented systems to produce them. My client then compared the actual cost percentage on the Profit and Loss statement with the targeted cost percentage from Little Caesars. When they were in line, he gave praises to his managers and team members. When they were off more than one percent, he investigated to solve the problem. This is how important a properly created Profit and Loss statement can be to your business.

Make sure that you take the time to create an accounting system that ensures all sales dollars are deposited into the bank. It is enough of a challenge to get and keep customers coming back. I personally like a daily sales summary that balances to a daily deposit. The daily sales are proved by Z tapes or invoices. Any cash paid-outs are listed on the daily summary. The balance is listed as bank deposit and that exact amount is deposited into the bank. Don't have the same person prepare the daily sales summary then make the bank deposits. You'll be asking for trouble in accounting for your money.

Take the time to create a future Profit and Loss statement. Sometimes this is called a Forecasted Profit and Loss Statement. This is important to decide that if you continue to do what you are doing now, that you will be happy or unhappy with the results. Whatever is in the past you can't change, but whatever is in the future you can.

Create a Budgeted Profit and Loss Statement. Work with your management team to decide what should be spent yearly, monthly, weekly, daily or even hourly based on revenue changes. Manage by budget and you will most likely get the budgeted profits that you show on your statement. This is simple but not easy. Whoever said that running a business is easy has probably never run a business before! When you find that there is a good reason for going over or under budget, change your Budgeted Profit and Loss Statement to recalculate the results. Hopefully the new results are acceptable to you as the business owner.

Another very important statement to track is the Return on your Marketing Investment. You need to capture the sales data that specifically came from each advertising campaign. To arrive at Return on Investment, you divide sales from each advertising campaign by the cost of each advertising campaign. An example of this method was provided in Business Secret #16 with the pizza shop.

For ease of understanding the effectiveness of your team members' handling of important procedures, you need to create a ratio or number. I call this an accountability measure.

I created an accountability measure called the Comp Ratio at Larry's Villa and Larry's Hideaway. It quickly helped me decide if the bartender was giving away too many free drinks to gamblers. Whatever major problem you have in your current business, try to quantify the effectiveness by creating your own accountability measure.

Consider outsourcing your accounting system. Here are eight reasons to outsource:

- Saves time and money in training you or your in-house bookkeeper or accountant.
- Studies show that you will gain 150-200 hours per year by outsourcing your accounting system.

- By saving time, you can focus your strengths as a business owner by growing your business and your money.
- There will be no need to buy, install, or monitor additional computer and bookkeeping software. You will never have to worry about losing your data.
- You will get your financial information on time and all IRS and state reports that are necessary will be accurately and timely filed.
- Be confident with the amount of money that you have banked at any given time because your bank balance is continually reconciled with your bank statements.
- You will gain access to much stronger accounting abilities and experience than most in-house accountants will have.
- Any government-imposed penalties for inaccurate or untimely reports would be paid by your outsourced accountant, not by you.

BUSINESS SECRET #28

BECOME EXCELLENT AT SELLING

Why does the business owner have to be excellent at selling? Can't the business owner just delegate that off to another team member? Why does the business owner need to be excellent at selling when he just rings up products at his retail store's cash register? Why does the business owner need to be excellent at selling when he is actively managing his service business and quoting the prices himself? I think you may even have more questions.

The better you are at selling, the more profitable your business will be. This is true even if you are not in direct contact with your clients or customers. If you are in charge of hiring the team members, you need to be excellent at selling in order to hire the best team members possible. If you are in purchasing or accounts receivable, you need to be excellent at selling to get the best price from your vendors and quickest payments received from your customers or clients. If you are in management, you need to be excellent at selling to get the most efficiency out of your team members. Excellent selling is involved in all aspects of your business.

David Sandler cut through the confusion on effective selling. He passed on many years ago, but his ideas are still as relevant today as ever. In fact, I am currently being coached in the David Sandler-style of selling right now.

David Mattson and Bruce Seidman wrote the book, *Sandler Success Principles: 11 Insights that will change the way you Think and Sell.*

They enlightened me in this book with how the actions of a nurturing parent, adult parent or critical parent can affect business and personal relationships. Let me explain these types of actions:

Nurturing Parent is a parent that reassures, comforts and supports their child. This type of parent is agreeable, approachable and communicates in a positive way. Nurturing Parent messages are likely to evoke OK emotions in the other person. People are more likely to interact effectively and communicate better with each other when they feel OK.

Critical Parent is a parent that tells the other person what should happen, what he or she should do, and what's right and wrong, appropriate and inappropriate, good and bad about his or her decisions, opinions and actions. Don't be surprised when the prospect decides to put a stop to the not-OK feelings by putting a stop to communications with you.

Adult Parent is a parent that brings some structure and a voice of patience, reason, logic, objectivity and experience to the conversation. They will be asking questions to make sure they are helping with the right problem.

On average, 30% of selling will come when you are in the Adult Parent mode. 70% of the selling will come when you are in the Nurturing Parent mode. 0% of the selling will come when you are in the Critical Parent mode.

Try to think of the last time that someone was in Critical Parent mode, telling you exactly what you should be doing, and you bought their idea or product completely. I'm sure you can't think of a time when that happened. Now think of a time when someone was in Nurturing Parent mode and was positively helping you decide what you would like to do. Most people likely followed what they were talking about.

I had never thought about this until I read this book. I asked some friends if I was a Critical

Parent-type and they told me I was! I've been trying hard to be much more nurturing and positive in my relationships and found amazing success from it. Try it! It might work for you.

Listen to your Prospects much more than you talk. Try to let your prospect speak three times more than you speak to them. You will be considered a great conversationalist and will build rapport much quicker in this fashion. How can you really find out what they need if you do most of the talking? There is a time to present your product or service and that is not when you are asking a series of questions to understand your prospects needs.

Sandler's, *You Can't Teach a Kid to Ride a Bike at a Seminar* book can help you understand how to uncover your prospect's pain.

Ask them questions that will uncover the emotions that will lead them to buy. In other words, find the pain that needs to be solved.

Ask:

- What is the business problem that keeps you up at night right now?
- What do you fear about the future for your business?
- What pleasures has your business given you in the past?
- What is the one thing that would please you the most about the operation of your future business?
- What are you curious or interested about in your business?

Ask Questions, Get Sales: Close the Deal and Create Long-Term Relationships is a book written by Stephan Schiffman that helps you create questions to understand your prospects much better.

Selling is finding out what people do and ways to do it better. Here are some great questions to ask your prospect:

- What do you do?
- What are your goals?
- How do you do it?
- When or where do you do it?
- Why do you do it that way?
- Who are you doing it with?
- How can we help you do it better?

- How are you going to choose who you'll be working with?
- Why did you decide to call us today?
- How are you going to use our service or products that you're looking for?
- What exactly is your company trying to accomplish?
- Have you ever worked with a company like ours before?
- How do you think we should get started?
- Where should we go from here?

One of the most important components of selling your products or services is your ability to get your prospect to know, like and trust you. Without establishing this, you probably won't close your sale. Building rapport is another way of saying that you want to get your prospect to know, like and trust you.

The Magic of Rapport: How You can Gain Personal Power in any Situation is a book written by Jerry Richardson. This book can help you learn how to better connect with your prospects quicker. Mirror or pace your prospect's speaking style, volume, speed of speaking, mannerisms or even body language to help build rapport quicker.

Dan Caramanico and Marie Maguire have written *The Optimal Salesperson: Mastering the Mindset of Sales Superstars and Overachievers.* This book can help you become a salesperson that creates new sales consistently. Here are its main tools to succeed:

- Create a Sales Activity Plan that tracks your sales activity goals daily, weekly and monthly.
- Create a Prospecting plan or program.
- Create and use an effective Sales Process.
- Keep improving your interpersonal skills.

Some obstacles to sales success are:

- Having self-limiting beliefs like believing that price is your prospects main concern, when really you know that prospects buy when value is higher than price.
- When you need approval from prospect or want to be liked instead of realizing that selling is more important.
- Reluctance to talk about money.
- A tolerance for excessive comparison shopping of your product or service.
- Not having a compelling reason to succeed – remember, you have to motivate yourself.

Secrets of Closing Sales: Contains the famous Master Closing Formula that can double or triple your sales income is a helpful book written by Charles B. Roth and Roy Alexander. Overcoming objections is certainly one of the ideas that you can learn in this book that will help you close more sales. Here are the eight ways that you can overcome the price objection:

1. Enhance the customer's sense of security by providing a time frame.
2. Remove the price issue by linking cost to customer's prime needs.
3. Take blame away from the prospect.
4. Make a conversational concession.
5. Agree that others felt the same way.
6. Compliment the prospect's idea.
7. Blame insufficient information.
8. Get on their side of the desk.

My father, Ron Howard, who is now 80 years young, was my salesman for about 10 years at BHI. I am much honored that he took his time to help me and my business become successful. He helped about 850 Las Vegas small businesses understand that they needed bookkeeping, payroll and/or income tax services and that BHI Bookkeeping was the best place to have those services handled for them.

His main training source was Zig Ziglar's epic book, *Secrets of Closing the Sale*. Now that he is retired and I'm starting to do the selling myself, he gave me his copy of the book. I enjoyed seeing how my father underlined phrases and learned from this book.

Thanks, Dad.

"If you give to others without measuring, you'll get repaid without ever asking for it" is a quote by author Robert S. Littell. He wrote the book entitled, *The Heart and Art of NetWeaving: Building Meaningful Relationships One Connection At a Time*. He suggests that you ask four key, probing questions to prospects that you meet:

1. Would you tell me how you make money?
2. What does a good prospect for you look like?
3. In business, family or personal context, what is your most burning problem, need or desire?
4. What is your strategic advantage?

Absorb and understand these answers and then help the prospects that you meet. The outcome will surprise you.

Then you'll start acting as a NetWeaver - Littell's term for people who've learned to listen with a second pair of ears, as well as a second set of antennas.

When you are thinking in the mindset as a "NetWorker", you would ask yourself whether someone is a potential prospect for you and if they can be of help to you.

When you are thinking in the mindset of a NetWeaver, you would ask yourself the following questions:

- Is there someone I know who would benefit from knowing this person?
- Are there resources this person could provide some of my clients or prospects?
- Are they a possible Trusted Resource Candidate?

On the next page is the NetWeaver's Creed.

The NetWeaver's Creed

- I will constantly be on the lookout for opportunities to put people together in win/win relationships without concern for what I will get out of it.

- I will shift from thinking about WIIFM (What's In It For ME) to WIIFY (What's In It For YOU).

- I will learn to be a resource for others, both regarding the types of information I can provide as well as to surround myself with resource contacts who can be of service to those with whom I come in contact.

- I will apply the principles of NetWeaving on a daily basis and will make a habit of doing those things that will allow me to best implement NetWeaving strategies.

- I will become an outspoken "NetWeaving" ambassador realizing that this will not only help others learn the joys and benefits of NetWeaving but that it will reflect positively back on me as well.

Bob Littell
Chief NetWeaver

BUSINESS SECRET #29

BE A LEADER

Just because you are in charge of your business, does that make you are a leader? There is so much more to being a leader than just having the leadership position. Do you think that if you just tell your team members to always complete a defined duty, they will do it, because if they don't, they will lose their job? When you take the time to check to see if that duty was accomplished, you may be surprised that parts of that defined duty were not accomplished.

Your business will have much more success when you lead and inspire your team members to greatness instead of just telling them what to do. Do *you* enjoy just being told what to do? Most people don't, and might find a way to disregard or adjust parts of the duty to their liking just so they don't feel like they were ordered to do so.

Fish! A Remarkable Way to Boost Morale and Improve Results is a book written by Stephen C.

Jundin, Ph.D., Harry Paul and John Christensen. It talks about how Seattle's Pike Place Fish Market was transformed from a failing business into a profitable business. New management decided that they needed to change the attitudes of their team members to become more friendly, pleasant and happy. At the same time, they realized that working with fresh fish all day was really not a fun job. It took about a year to transform Pike's Place team, but it happened.

The leaders of Pike's Place started by sharing ideas with their team members and asked how to make working more fun. They put up a sign that said, "Choose your Attitude" with one happy face and one frown face. They put up another sign that said, "There is always a choice about the way you do your work, even if there is not a choice about the work itself." The ideas for signs came from the team members. The leaders made sure they shared with the team who came up with what idea.

The next idea team members came up with was to throw the fish around to each other in the market. The team members had fun with it and so did the customers. They put up another sign that said, "This is a Playground. Watch out for Adult Children."

Here are the benefits of Play:

- Happy people treat others well.

- Fun leads to creativity.
- Time passes quickly.
- Having a good time is healthy.
- Work becomes a reward and not just a way to rewards.

It's Your Ship: Management Techniques from the Best Damn Ship in the Navy is a book written by Captain D. Michael Abrashoff.

You might think management problems and solutions are quite different between the Navy and your private sector business. Captain Abrashoff points out in his book that there are many systems that he implemented on the USS Benfold, one of the most technologically-advanced ships at the time but with low-productivity, that can be used quite effectively in both.

The top five reasons for leaving the Navy or any other type of employment are the same. Number Five on both lists was pay. The Number One reason for leaving the Navy showed that it was how personnel, known as Direct Reports, were personally treated. Was there room for personal growth, were they trusted to think on their own and were their ideas about improving operations actually implemented?

Why not start by asking your Direct Reports, "Why do we have to do it that way? Is there a better way?" You might be surprised what you will find out.

Had you ever considered that firing a Direct Report is really a failure of management? It usually is. Either management did not clearly articulate the problem or did not give Direct Reports enough time, materials or training.

Realize your influence over your Direct Reports. Take the time to learn who they are. See the Ship or Your Business through their eyes. Personally interview every Direct Report and know them as individuals.

In two years, Captain Abrashoff took a crew that was performing poorly with a 20% re-enlistment to leading the Navy with many records and 100% re-enlistment. Keep talking to your Direct Reports and keep them informed of what's in store for them. Find a common goal for everyone and you will end up with a crew that can do anything. Take personal pleasure as the manager to help others recognize their own strengths. Consider an after-action critic circle to learn from the crew's actions. Let your crew feel as though they can speak freely.

Never tear down your Direct Reports. Try to anticipate what they will want before they know. If all you give is orders, then all you will ever get is order-takers. Bet on that people will think for themselves. Find ways to get your people cross-trained and challenge your crew beyond its reach.

Help them grow strong.

John C. Maxwell wrote the book, *Leadership 101: What Every Leader Needs to Know.* Most businesses owners stand alone due to their ego, insecurity, naiveté and temperament. Woodrow Wilson said, "We should not only use the brains we have, but also use the brains that we can borrow." Teamwork divides the effort and multiplies the effect.

Here are 10 steps to building a team:

1. Make the decision to build a team. It starts with the individual.
2. Gather the best team possible. It elevates the potential of your team.
3. Pay the price to develop the team. Realize that it will ensure growth.
4. Do things together as a team. It provides community.
5. Empower team members with responsibility and authority. This raises up leaders for the team.
6. Give credit to the team for the success of the team.
7. Watch to see that the Investment in team pays off. This brings accountability to the team.
8. Take the blame and never the credit.
9. Create opportunities for the team. This allows the team to stretch.

10. Give the team the best possible chance to succeed.

Get involved today and create small and big teams in your business. Lyndon B. Johnson said, "There is no problem too big we can't solve together and very few we can solve ourselves." Get your issues solved in your business by getting everyone in your business (Your Team) involved and working together. It is not easy, but it's worth the effort.

Lincoln on Leadership: Executive Strategies for Tough Times was written by Donald T. Phillips. This book has some amazingly simple ideas to become the leader that you need to be to increase your business's success. Here are some of his ideas:

- Choose as your chief subordinates those people who crave responsibility and will take risks.
- Go out into the field with your leaders, and stand or fall with the battle.
- If employees gripe about one of your chief supervisors, and the complaints are true, do not be afraid to remove him.
- Never crush a man out, thereby making him and his friends permanent enemies of your organization.
- No purpose is served by punishing merely for punishment's sake

- Touch people with the better angels of your nature.
- When you make it to the top, turn and reach down for the person behind you.
- Remember that your followers generally want to believe that what they do is their own idea and, more importantly, that it genuinely makes a difference.

You Don't Need a Title to Be a Leader: How Anyone, Anywhere, Can Make a Positive Difference is a book written by Mark Sanborn. A leader acts in the following ways:

- They believe that they can positively shape lives and careers.
- They lead through relationships with people as opposed to their control over people.
- They collaborate with people instead of control people.
- They persuade others to contribute, rather than order them to complete duties.
- They get others to follow them out of respect and commitment rather than through fear and compliance.

Here are the differences between Leaders and Managers:

- Managers have employees and Leaders win followers.

- Managers react to change and Leaders create change.
- Managers have good ideas and Leaders implement them.
- Managers communicate and Leaders persuade.
- Managers direct groups and Leaders create teams.
- Managers try to be heroes and Leaders make heroes of everyone around them.
- Managers take credit and Leaders take responsibility.
- Managers exercise power over people and Leaders exercise power with people.

The One Minute Manager Meets the Monkey: Don't Take on the Problem if the Problem Isn't Yours. That Monkey Doesn't Belong to You! is a book co-authored by Kenneth Blanchard, William Oncken and Hal Burrows.

The more you take care of everything for other people, the more dependent they become on you. Their self-confidence is eroded and they will be prevented from taking care of your own Monkeys. A Monkey is the *Next Move* in action you need to accomplish. For every Monkey there are two parties involved: one to work it and one to supervise it.

Rules of Monkey Management

Rule 1: *Descriptions* – The "next moves" are specified.

Rule 2: *Owners* – The Monkey is assigned to a person.

Rule 3: *Insurance Policies* – The risk is covered. Recommend, and then act. Act and then advise.

Rule 4: *Monkey Feeding and Checkup Appointments* – The time and place for follow-up is specified.

The best way to develop responsibility in people is to give them responsibility. The purpose of coaching team members is to get into the position to delegate to them. I can't delegate until my anxieties allow it. I can delegate only if I am reasonably sure my people know what is to be done. It would be foolish to delegate to someone without reasonable assurance that he or she can get sufficient resources such as time, information, money, people, assistance and authority to do the work. Don't delegate the duty unless everything is present for them to succeed.

BUSINESS SECRET #30

POSITIVE REINFORCEMENT

You have heard of Positive Reinforcement, right? Do you know how to apply it? Do you realize the power it has to help people working with you toward your goals? You can get the behavior you want by using positive reinforcement.

Let's say it is Spring outside. Yeah! Spring is here. You should be happy! It always feels like another new beginning. Just like Spring comes back every year, every *day* you have the opportunity to start again. Aren't we all lucky that we can do that? Yes, we are!

Discover the powers of Positive Reinforcement and its amazing abilities to help change behavior for the better. It really works!

Positive Reinforcement can affect behavior in relationships such as: Employee/Employer,

Employer/Employee, Parent/Child, Child/Parent, Any Family member/Any Family member, to as many other relationships you can think of.

You may say that you have a positive outlook on life and therefore you've already apply positive reinforcement in your relationships. Imagine what could happen if you were educated in how to apply positive reinforcement. Wow!

What would happen if your attitude changed from TGIF (Thank God It's Friday) work days to TGIM (Thank God It's Monday)? This can happen with the help of you and your relationships.

I had always thought that if I set penalties and punishments for my Employer/Employee relationships, that my employees would follow the rules. In reality, the only rules my employees followed were those that they knew had certain punishments associated with it for **not** following my rules. Penalties and Punishment philosophies do not work!

I suggest to everyone to find positive behaviors in your relationships, and then tell them, "You did great!" Tell them again a little later about something else they did great. Repeat! Repeat! Repeat! This is Positive Reinforcement!

A friend of mine told me about his wife who he loved very much and had been married to for over

30 years. She had put on a little extra weight over the years. He noticed that she'd made some small strides into losing a few pounds. Instead of telling her she needed to work harder at losing more weight, he praised her for her smaller efforts. The more he praised her, the harder she worked on her own, and eventually lost those extra pounds. She looked fantastic in the process.

Aubrey C. Daniels wrote, *Bringing out the Best in People: How to Apply the Astonishing Power of Positive Reinforcement.*

Here are some ideas from the book:

- Effective leaders positively reinforce behaviors while team members are performing the task.
- There should be about four praises to every constructive criticism. Too much praise or too little praise will lose it effectiveness.
- Track your attempts at Positive Reinforcement.
- Positive Reinforce the small improvements toward the bigger goal.
- Hourly is the best feedback time interval, but at the very least, positive reinforce daily.
- Don't sandwich your praise around a constructive criticism. Your team members will only hear the constructive criticism.
- When you must constructively criticize a team member, only tell them how to do it

better. Don't also tell them what they did great.
- Only praise by itself. Try to praise in short amounts of time, like one minute. Get team members to look forward to seeing you. They are expecting more praise from you.
- Pinpoint the exact specific results that are needed to accomplish the task. Don't tell team members what not to do. Tell team members what to do.
- When instructing team members, try the Morningside Academy methods of teaching that resulted in an average 2.5 grade knowledge increase per year. They used 10 minutes of instruction, 40 minutes of practice and 10 minutes of break.

BUSINESS SECRET #31

RESULTS-BASED ADVERTISING

What do you want to accomplish by investing your money into advertising? Will you know if your advertising campaign is successful? Do you know what the return on investment is for each advertising campaign? Do you A/B test the same advertisement with small differences to see which advertisement brings in more sales dollars? Did you realize there are ways to test the effectiveness of your advertising campaign before you launch it?

One common need for most businesses is that they want more customers. They decide they just need to get the word out, and so they look for some form of advertising. Maybe an advertising salesman contacts them at the right time when sales are dropping and offers to bring new customers with their specific platform like radio, television, mailers, websites, texting, emailing, flyers and more. They make it easy for the businessman because they will even create the ad for them. After spending the money on advertisement, the businessman is usually unhappy with the results. This cycle repeats itself daily in the United States.

How do I know this? I know this because I have hired as many of these people as I can possibly find. I hired them when I ran for political office in Las Vegas in five different races. I hired them to help to bring in new customers for Rancho Home Center, Larry's Hideaway, Larry's Villa and BHI Bookkeeping. I started to notice similar results in all of my advertising activities.

I had to be much more knowledgeable about creating and monitoring the effectiveness of my marketing campaigns. I hired several marketing coaches to help me improve. After all, there are many businesses that are successful in growing their business whether the overall economy is growing or contracting.

Bradley J. Sugars wrote an amazing book entitled, *Instant Promotions: Instant Success, Real Results. Right Now.* What you need is an attractive Headline to the reader. Know your target audience so that you will know what excites them. You can find out what excites them by asking your current customers why they buy from you. Add a sub-headline that explains the headline further. Don't tell your entire story in the ad. Spend more time to create the idea in the lowest number of words possible. Use pictures and not graphic art to catch the attention of the reader. Create a great offer to the reader. Put in a deadline or expiration date.

The next page shows examples of great ad formats.

Most small businesses write ads with their name as the most important focal point of the ad. It isn't. The most important focal point is the headline, offer or compelling reason to read the ad further. Pictures will grab the reader's attention and next, the caption of the pictures. Notice how the offer is repeated in the ad. Notice how the company's name and contact information is at the bottom of the ad and in very small type. What is the point of knowing your business's name or contact information if the reader is not interested in your headline, offer or compelling reasons to buy your service or product? The reader should also be able to scan your ad without reading it to get the main ideas. If the reader wants more information, they can read the text.

Here are some examples of powerful offers:

- **Free Haircut** – A hairdressing salon looking to increase its database.
- **Two Steak Dinners and Two Glasses of Wine for $10** – For a restaurant recruiting members for its VIP Club.
- **One New Release Video and a Large Pizza for $3** – A video store promotion to recruit new members.

Here are some examples of weak offers:

- **10 % Off** – Not big enough of a discount to generate interest. This ad would also depend upon the size of the purchase.
- **Call Now for Your Free Color Brochure** – So what? Everyone hands out brochures. Unless the product is something incredible, people won't respond.
- **Buy 9 and Get the 10th for Half Price** – No one would respond to this offer. It's too small.

Here are types of offers that would be worth considering:

- **The Added Value with Soft Dollar Costs** – Find a high-perceived value that you can combine with your product or service that doesn't cost too much to increase sales of your products or services.
- **The Package Offer** – Customers will buy more just because they are packaged together even when the packaged price equals the total of the sale prices of everything in the package.
- **Discounts vs. Bonus Offers** – "Two for the Price of One" sale or "Buy One and Get One FREE" are examples of this type of offer.

- **Valued-at Offer** – "Call now for your FREE consultation, valued at $75" is an example of this type of offer.
- **Time-Limited Offers** – Make sure that you have a time limit or expiration date on your offer or your customer has no reason to come in now.
- **Guaranteed Offers** – People will be far more willing to part with their money if you take the risk out of the buying decision.

Forecast or estimate the total gross profit that has to increase as a direct result of investing in your proposed advertising campaign. Gross profit is your sales less your direct cost of the sale, such as product or increased labor costs. If gross profits aren't substantially more than the costs of your proposed advertising campaign, don't do it unless you can acquire the new customers contact information, and the new customers long-term value is much more than the cost of the advertising campaign.

Long-term value of a customer is calculated by estimating out how many times they will buy from your business in their lifetime times the average dollar amount of purchases they buy. If you estimate the customer will buy from you 20 times and spend on average $20 each time, the long-term value of a customer is $400.

Bradley J. Sugars wrote *Instant Leads: Instant Success, Real Results. Right Now.* He has some great ideas on how to make a successful radio campaign. Here are four important points:

1. **Targeted Demographic.** You don't want to advertise on a station where the listening audience is of an age or gender that would not be interested in your product or service.
2. **Sound Effects.** Use sound effects at the beginning of your radio ad to grab attention. Use a scream, bang a gong, car crash, silence, the word attention, breaking news, or anything else that will grab their attention.
3. **Copy.** Once your sound effects have attracted the attention of your listener, you need to convey the benefits of buying your product or service in a clear, believable, and easy-to-understand fashion.
4. **Music.** Your music should appeal to the target you're aiming at and it should complement the product or service you're trying to sell.

A 30-second commercial only has between 65 to 85 words to work with. Choose your words carefully. Your opening line is your headline and needs to be a powerful headline or offer. Find the right "voice" for your ad that matches what you want to present to the listener.

   Make sure that you have a Call to Action in your radio ad or any type of ad or promotion that you create. This is something like, *Call today, Buy today or Come on in today*.

   At BHI Bookkeeping, I recently put a simple electrical moving sign outside that says, *Come on in Today* and people have been coming in more often.

   Here is an example of a *suggestive* radio ad that I'm sure would grab your attention for a new bedding store:

   The commercial starts with a man and woman grunting and groaning in the bedroom. He asks her to slide it in gently while he holds her end. The moaning then gets louder and louder until finally she says, "I give up. We're never going to get this sheet to fit." An announcer then comes on and explains that if you need new sheets, you should go and see ZXY Bedding.

   Here is another example of an effective radio commercial for Charlie's Garage:

- **Special Effects** – First you hear a whip cracking and cows mooing.

173

- **First Voice** – Yeeeehah! It's Sheriff Charlie here, back in town lookin' to lynch crook tires.
- **First Voice** – Now we all know that crook tires are killers. So I'm offerin' up a reward for anyone who rustles up a couple of varmints.
- **First Voice** – If you run in two or more crook tires, I'll give you $20 towards the cost of your new tires.
- **First Voice** – So mosey on in now to Sheriff Charlie's Garage, corner of Smith and Dominion Roads. Help me lynch those crook tires.

We all know that one of the most effective ways to increase new customers is through referrals. But how can we increase the numbers of referrals we get? The answer is by creating Strategic Alliances with non-competitive businesses that are already dealing with your target market of customers. Try to find these non-competitive businesses that have a large database and whose customers already like them. They need to be in the same end of quality and price and have a willingness to test new marketing ideas.

You can offer your new strategic alliance a large commission and offer to send new customers to them so they know they are sending referrals to the best business possible. At the end of each sales presentation, you could ask a series of questions of other needs that your prospect might want that are the type of businesses that you have already set up strategic alliances with.

Another great way to get new referrals from your new strategic alliances is through a free gift of your product or service. This letter would be written for the strategic alliance by you as though they were writing it. You could print and mail it for the strategic alliance with their approval. It could be as simple as the following:

Thanks for being a customer of ours. We really appreciate it. Just to show you how truly grateful we are, we've arranged a special gift for you - a complimentary Style Cut with Julia's Hairdressing. We recommend Julia's Hairdressing highly and are certain you'll appreciate how fantastic your hair will look.

Imagine how your customers will feel about the free gift that was given to them. It will remind them that you care and these customers will also come back more often to your business. This means increased customers to both strategic alliance partners.

BUSINESS SECRET #32

JUST DO IT

Isn't that the Nike slogan? Yes, it is. It is so simple yet so effective. I applaud your efforts for reading my book. It's certainly an effort towards Just Doing It. I can't remember how many books I have read that stated something similar to this motto. By reading and getting great advice from expert coaches, you are getting the basis for success. But without *doing it*, your knowledge won't really matter to you except to build your confidence. Your confidence can start to drop if you don't see the success you want to have.

It is also possible that you keep investing your time and resources into knowledge and skill training because you have a fear that maybe your new abilities won't be successful. **Don't fear failure.** Thomas Edison failed more than 10,000 times in his quest to create the electric light bulb. He wasn't worried though. After each failure, he figured at least he'd found another way that it wouldn't work and was a little closer to creating it.

Wayne Allyn Root wrote *The Joy of Failure! How to Turn Failure, Rejection and Pain into Extraordinary Success.* Here are the five power principles and positive addictions that will help you design the life of your dreams:

1. Do It with Attitude!
2. Do It Today!
3. Do It with Style!
4. Do It Boldly!
5. Do It with Others!

Here are some great quotes from his book:

- *"Only those who dare to fail greatly can ever achieve greatly."* John F. Kennedy
- *"In the middle of difficulty lies opportunity."* Albert Einstein
- *"Life is either a daring adventure or nothing."* Helen Keller
- *"Victims complain, survivors settle, THRIVERS rule the world!"* Wayne Allyn Root
- *"The things which hurt, instruct."* Benjamin Franklin
- *"Nothing great will ever be achieved without great men and men are great only if they are determined to be so."* Charles de Gaulle

177

- *"A good plan violently executed now is far better than a perfect plan next week."* George S. Patton
- *"Experience is the name everyone gives to their mistakes."* Oscar Wilde
- *"Our greatest glory is not in never falling, but in rising every time we fail."* Confucius

Don't worry about failure. Just Do It!

ABOUT THE AUTHOR

I have always received the most enjoyment in my life from what I call "Turning on the Light Bulb". This is when I'm trying to do something and then it works. The following are some of these "Turning on the Light Bulb" situations:

- When I was coaching my daughter (Chrystal) in soccer how to play defense and then she just made an amazing defensive take away in the game on their best player.
- When I created a co-ed adult softball team where everyone plays equally and our weakest player just got a hit to score a run.
- After I had been coaching my daughter (Cassidy) in basketball for many years and she beat me in a game of 21.
- I learned how to two-step from my dance instructor, Dane, and my wife, Lisa, over a couple of years. Lisa and I went country dancing at Gilley's on her birthday.

- Afterwards, she told me I was the best two-stepper out there. Of course it helps a lot to have a great dance partner.
- When I created my own country band called "The Sunday Guys" and the customers kept coming back to enjoy our style of music at Larry's Hideaway.
- When having music lessons to play the guitar better, my teacher showed me how to play a "lick" that was on a BB King song and I played it like the record.
- When I studied to take the test to become an insurance agent and I passed it the first time even though I had never been in this business.
- When I needed to figure out how to hire an amazing salesman for my bookkeeping business and was able to hire my dad, Ron Howard. He was able to help over 850 small businesses that they really needed our services.
- When I was able to find ways to get my entire family over for a Sunday dinner for many years.
- When I was able to make sure that my mother, LeAnne Howard, was on the sidelines for almost all of the sporting

events that my two daughters were involved in for over 15 years.
- When I was able to figure out the next great idea to try to help the people of Las Vegas by trying to get elected to public office.
- When I figured out how to write and publish my own monthly newsletter for BHI Bookkeeping.
- When I was finally able to talk my sister, Lori Howard, into working with me.
- When I was able to hire an amazing accountant, Dan Nitchie, who is also my good friend to work with me at BHI Bookkeeping who has been with me for 20 years.
- When I was able to suggest to my son-in-law, Dan Skougard, that he could be a really good DJ at Larry's Hideaway and he decided to do it. He is still a great DJ to this day.
- When I was able to buy my commercial building and figured out how to design and remodel it.
- When I was finally able to talk my longtime best friends, Steve and Laurie Clemens, into starting their own computer learning school and they did it.

- When I figured out how to represent myself in court and win the case.
- When I learned the next amazing idea from a book, a coach, CD, video, webinar or seminar and when I put it into action and it worked.
- When I figured out how to set S.M.A.R.T. goals in regards to losing weight and it worked.
- When I was able to help my longtime friend, Paul Deyo, believe that he could work at a job that he never thought he would be able to do.
- When I have given a business idea to a client, he used it and it worked.

Of course there are many more….

Brent Howard has lived in Las Vegas, Nevada since 1964.

BRENT D. HOWARD

2385 North Decatur Blvd. Cellular: (702) 501-2204
Las Vegas, Nevada 89108 Office: (702) 259-9983
E-Mail: Brenth2009@gmail.com Fax: (702) 259-9962
Website: Las-Vegas-Business.com

SUMMARY OF EXPERTISE

~ Over 34 Years as a *BUSINESS OWNER*.

~ Over 12 Years as a *LICENSED INSURANCE AGENT*.

~ Expert in all facets of *OPERATIONS START-UP, MANAGEMENT & ADMINISTRATION*:

* Strategic Business Plans & Budgets
* Sales/Expense Forecasts & Projections
* Policy/Procedure Implementation/Administration
* Cost Analysis & Internal Controls
* Creative Organization & Operations Supervision
* Vendor Research
* Vendor Research & Resource Coordination
* Purchasing Management
* Inventory & Quality Controls
* Loss Prevention
* Report Preparation & Records Maintenance
* Personnel Recruitment & Staffing
* Tax Preparation & Reporting
* Bookkeeping Maintenance

~ Proficient skills in *MARKETING, ADVERTISING, PROMOTIONS & CUSTOMER SERVICE*:

* Marketing Research & Analysis

* Territory & Account Development
* Internet & Mass Media Advertising Campaigns
* Special Promotions

~ Computer Proficiency: Windows 7, Microsoft Word, Publisher, PowerPoint, Excel, Creative Solutions, Tax Slayer, Excel, QuickBooks, Quattro Pro, Barracuda Systems, Peachtree, DAC Easy & WordPerfect Software.

ACHIEVEMENTS

* Larry's Villa & Larry's Hideaway, 2011 Las Vegas Review Journal Newspaper "Best Of Las Vegas" Award
* Author, Business Success Paperback & eBook (Amazon.com)

LICENSES / CERTIFICATIONS

- Registered Tax Return Preparer IRS Certification: Active
- Property, Casualty, Annuity, Life & Health Insurance Sales License, State of Nevada: Active
- Series 6 & 63 Sales License, State of Nevada: Inactive

EDUCATIONAL BACKGROUND

University of Nevada, Las Vegas, Nevada
Nevada Insurance School, Las Vegas, Nevada
Bachelor Science Degree in Accounting
Property, Casualty, Annuity, Life & Health Insurance Sales Program &Licensure

Honors: Scholarship Recipient; Early Graduate

SPECIALTY TRAINING

- ~ Brent Howard Accounting & Computer Services, Inc., NV, NJ & CA: Dan Kennedy Marketing, Action Coach Business & Accounting and Universal & New Clients, Inc. Accounting Marketing Strategies; Nina Lewis Social Media & Writing Techniques.
- ~ Nevada Insurance Commission, Las Vegas, NV: Workers Compensation Audit, Laws & Litigation.
- ~ Clark County Assessor's Office, Las Vegas, NV: Property Assessment Rules & Regulations.

PROFESSIONAL EXPERIENCE

1978 - Present

BRENT HOWARD ACCOUNTING & COMPUTER SERVICES, INC.
(dba BHI Bookkeeping, Payroll & Income Tax and BHI Insurance Companies) - Las Vegas, Nevada

OWNER / OPERATOR
Established, owns and operates Full-Service Bookkeeping, Payroll, Tax and Insurance Companies with duties that include: Procuring licenses and permits; Designing plans, obtaining financing and overseeing remodel construction of 2,400 sq. ft. free-standing building; Creating Company Logos, Vision Statement and Sales Goals; Developing Annual Budgets with Sales Projections and Expense Forecasts; Utilizing direct mail and effective cold-calling techniques to generate new and referral clientele; retrieve and maintain client accounting files; Recruiting, hiring/firing, training, scheduling, assigning job duties, giving written evaluations, motivating, mentoring and supervising

employees to include Sales Associates, Accountants and Delivery Personnel; Following up, troubleshooting, resolving customer issues to ensure satisfaction and retention.

After creating enterprises with 1,000 clients and generating $1 million in annual revenue, expanded company into ***BUSINESS CONSULTANT FIRM*** providing services that include:

INDIVIDUAL ENTREPRENEURS/NEW START-UP BUSINESSES

Setting up partnership, LLC, Non-Profit or S-Corporation, determined by tax ramifications, and registering business with State of Nevada and federal agencies.

Assessing needs, helping create for Culture, Vision and Mission Statements and generating 3-5 Year Business Plans. Procuring start-up funding, licenses and facility leases as needed.
Creating Operating Budgets with Sales Projections and Expense Forecasts, newsletters as well as Strategic Marketing, Advertising and Promotional Plans to include Facebook, Twitter, LinkedIn, Foursquare and other Internet Optimization strategies.
Setting up Accounting Books, Charts of Accounts and Accountability Measure, Internal, Cost, Purchasing, Quality, Loss Prevention and Records Maintenance Controls.
Provide document pickup services, electronic backup of accounting records and audit representation.

ESTABLISHED BUSINESS/INDIVIDUAL ACCOUNTS

Providing updates on new laws, planning, preparing and filing Business, Self-Employment, Estimated Income, Corporate, Partnership, Personal Property, Sales and Payroll Taxes.

Preparing Annual Budgets, Sales Forecasts, Expense Projections, Financial, Profit, Loss and Income Statements, Executive and General Payroll to include: W-2/9/1099/940/941, Garnishments and IRS levies, as well as Commission, Expense, Accrual, Aging and Sales, Federal, State, Payroll Tax Reports.

Maintaining Charts of Accounts, General Ledgers, Accounts Receivable, Accounts.

Payable, Trial Balance, Bank and Trust Account Reconciliations.

Conducting Cost, Budget, Volume, Age Variance, Customer Hour Count & Efficiency analysis to calculate return on investment and business growth.

PAST AFFILIATIONS

* National Association of Tax Preparers: Two-Year Member
* Clark County Assessor's Office, Las Vegas, NV: 2010 Assessor Candidate
* Clark County Commissioner Office, Las Vegas, NV: 2008 Commissioner Candidate
* Nevada State Assembly #1: 2002, 2004 & 2006 Assembly Candidate
* Southern Nevada Youth Soccer, Las Vegas, NV: Treasurer; Coach – 10 years
* Bobby Socks, Las Vegas, NV: Softball Coach – 8 years
* YMCA, Las Vegas, NV: Basketball Coach – 6 years

~ Bondable
~ Willing To Travel

Professional and personal references provided on request

REFERENCES

Mastering the Rockefeller Habits
Verne Harnish

Grinding It Out: The Making of McDonalds
Ray Kroc

The Customer Comes Second
Hal F. Rosenbluth

The New Gold Standard
Joseph A. Michelli

The Starbucks Experience
Joseph A. Michelli

Good to Great
Jim Collins

World Famous
David Tyreman

Purple Cow
Seth Godin

Raving Fans
Ken Blanchard

Ice to the Eskimos
Jon Spoelstra

The Ultimate Marketing Plan
Dan S. Kennedy

No B.S. Price Strategy: The Ultimate No Holds Barred, Kick Butt, Take No Prisoners Guide to Profits, Power and Prosperity
Dan S. Kennedy

The New Relationship Marketing
Mari Smith

Facebook Marketing: An Hour a Day
Mari Smith

Social Media Marketing: An Hour a Day
Dave Evans

Twitter Marketing: An Hour a Day
Hollis Thomases

Social Boom! How to Master Business Social Media
Jeffrey Gitomer

Engage
Brian Solis

Permission Marketing
Seth Godin

Enchantment
Guy Kawasaki

Social Media the Fun Way!
Sandi Krakowski

Likeable Social Media
Dave Kerpen

Engagement Marketing, How Small Business Wins in a Socially Connected World
Gail F. Goodman

Build a Million Dollar Business in Las Vegas Richelle Shaw

You Can't Teach a Kid to Ride a Bike at a Seminar: The Sandler Sales Institute's 7-Step System for Successful Selling
David Sandler

Extraordinary Guarantees, Achieving Breakthrough Gains in Quality and Customer Satisfaction
Christopher W. Hart, Ph.D.

The Irresistible Offer: How to Sell Your Product or Service in 3 Seconds or Less
Mark Joyner

The Richest Man in Babylon
George S. Clason

8 Ways to Great: Peak Performance on the Job and in Your Life
Dr. Doug Hirschhorn

Who: The A Method for Hiring
Randy Street

Happier: Learn the Secrets to Daily Joy and Lasting Fulfillment
Tal Ben-Shahar, Ph.D.

Sandler Success Principles: 11 Insights that will change the way you Think and Sell
David Mattson and Bruce Seidman

Ask Questions, Get Sales: Close the Deal and Create Long-Term Relationships
Stephan Schiffman

The Magic of Rapport: How You can Gain Personal Power in any Situation
Jerry Richardson

The Optimal Salesperson: Mastering the Mindset of Sales Superstars and Overachievers
Dan Caramanico and Marie Maguire

Secrets of Closing Sales: Contains the famous Master Closing Formula that can double or triple your sales income
Charles B. Roth and Roy Alexander

Secrets of Closing the Sale
Zig Ziglar

The Heart and Art of NetWeaving: Building Meaningful Relationships One Connection At a Time
Robert S. Littell

Fish! A Remarkable Way to Boost Morale and Improve Results
Stephen C. Jundin, Ph.D., Harry Paul and John Christensen

Broken Windows, Broken Business
Michael Levine

It's Your Ship: Management Techniques from the Best Damn Ship in the Navy
Captain D. Michael Abrashoff

Leadership 101: What Every Leader Needs to Know
John C. Maxwell

Lincoln on Leadership: Executive Strategies for Tough Times
Donald T. Phillips

You Don't Need a Title to Be a Leader: How Anyone, Anywhere, Can Make a Positive Difference
Mark Sanborn

The One Minute Manager Meets the Monkey: Don't Take on the Problem if the Problem Isn't Yours. That Monkey Doesn't Belong to You!
Kenneth Blanchard, William Oncken and Hal Burrows

Bringing out the Best in People: How to Apply the Astonishing Power of Positive Reinforcement
Aubrey C. Daniels

Sales Magic: Increase your sales dramatically. Proven techniques by one of America's top sales and marketing experts
Steve Bryant

Five Minutes with VITO: Making the most of your selling time with the Very Important Top Officer
David Mattson and Anthony Parinello

Gen BuY: How Tweens, Teens, and Twenty-Somethings are Revolutionizing Retail
Kit Yarrow, Ph.D. and Jayne O'Donnell

The Power Formula for LinkedIn Success
Wayne Breitbarth

Instant Promotions: Instant Success, Real Results. Right Now
Bradley J. Sugars

Instant Leads: Instant Success, Real Results. Right Now
Bradley J. Sugars

The Joy of Failure! How to Turn Failure, Rejection and Pain into Extraordinary Success
Wayne Allyn Root

Made in the USA
Charleston, SC
13 November 2012